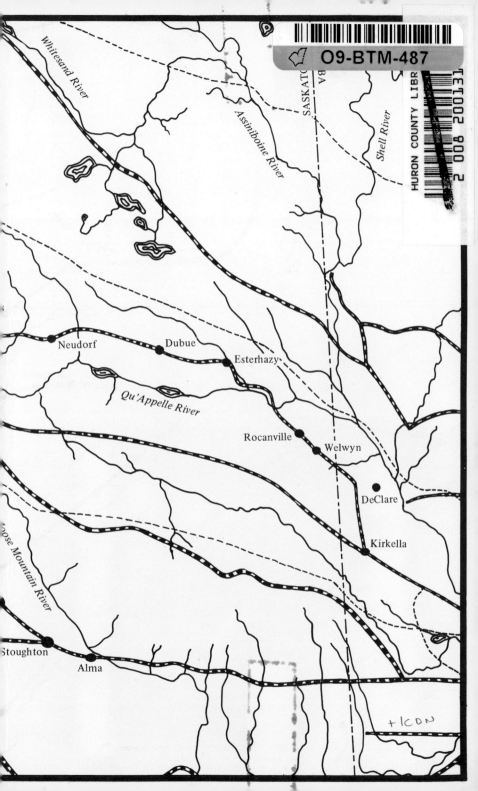

Whitesand River

Assiniboine River

SASKATO

BA

Shell River

Neudorf

Dubue

Esterhazy

Qu'Appelle River

Rocanville

Welwyn

DeClare

Kirkella

oose Mountain River

Stoughton

Alma

+ICDN

END OF STEEL

D. E. MACINTYRE

41676

PETER MARTIN ASSOCIATES LIMITED

Acknowledgements

For assistance in the preparation of this book, my grateful thanks are due to the following people for the information they supplied in such generous fashion. Without their help I could not have completed this work.

Mr. W. I. Smith, Dominion Archivist, Ottawa, and his staff.
Miss Juliette Bourque, Chief Librarian, Archives Library.
Mrs. Marion Beyea, Public Archives, Toronto.
Mr. John Stiff, Department of Mines and Northern Affairs, Toronto.
Mrs. Tillie Tobin (Macdonald), Cornwall, Ontario.
Mrs. Dorothy Smith, author of *Up and Down the Glen,* Alexandria, Ontario.
Mr. O.S.A. Lavalée, Canadian Pacific Railway Public Relations, Montreal.
Mr. E. N. Mainprize, C.P. Services, Ottawa.
Mr. S. S. Wothern, Editor, *Canadian Rail,* Montreal.
Mr. Thomas C. Main, P. Eng., former CPR surveyor, Wakefield, Quebec.
Mrs. Frank L. Packard, author of *The Reluctant Pioneer,* Montreal.
Mr. H. E. Wright, Principal, Montreal High School.
Mr. Andrew Collard, author, Montreal *Gazette.*
Mr. Duncan H. DuFresne, Canadian Railroad Historical Association.
Mrs. Marjorie Barber, Chelsea, Quebec, who typed the manuscript.

Photographs pages 64c–64h courtesy of the Public Archives of Canada.

© 1973 D.E. Macintyre

ISBN 0-88778-068-7

Printed in Canada by Readers' Club of Canada Ltd.

Design: S. Fothergill and D. McElroy

Peter Martin Associates Limited
35 Britain St., Toronto M5A 1R7, Ontario

CONTENTS

PREFACE

A boy was lucky to be born in Montreal in the last years of the nineteenth century. In 1885, when I was born, it was a small city of 178,000 people and we saw the last of a way of life that Montrealers had lived since the first settlers came to Canada's future metropolis.

Signs of the great changes that were about to overtake the whole civilized world were beginning to appear. The newspapers and magazines were publishing sensational articles about the wonders that were awaiting us in the new century.

The French author Jules Verne, with his fertile imagination, was writing stories about people flying in the air, travelling to the moon, navigating under the sea and going around the world in eighty days. Only a prophet could have known that some of his fantastic conceptions were about to come true.

About the year 1900, a few citizens actually had telephones. We had the only one on our street, but we were forced to take it out because so many people wanted to use it. Street railways were operating on tracks, even though horses supplied the traction. A few daring men were claiming that they could make a machine that would fly under its own power, while eminent scientists proved by mathematics that it was impossible for a machine of the proposed weight to get off the ground. (They were right by their standards, but they were calculating on using a coal-fired steam engine. The internal-combustion motor fired by gasoline had not yet been produced.) Cities were lighted by gas lamps, every one of which had to be ignited each evening by a man with a lighter. But a better arc light powered by electricity was making its appearance on some of our principal streets. Travel to the moon was a subject that was treated with derision. Other enthusiasts were tinkering with a horseless carriage, an idea that was ridiculed not only in the comic papers but in the best magazines. Nothing, they claimed, could compare with a well-bred and groomed horse and a smartly turned-out carriage equipped with rubber-tired wheels. Even the pneumatic rubber tire was a new idea; my first bicycle had hard, narrow rubber tires.

The astonishing feature about the great scientific and technological changes that have taken place in the twentieth century is that they happened so recently that millions of people now living were born and grew to maturity, understanding life as it was in the nineteenth and early twentieth centuries.

No such rapid and world-wide evolution has ever before occurred in the history of man.

I shall try in the following pages to depict some aspects of life as it was lived in Canada within my memory and well before the First World War.

1 OLD MONTREAL

While inventors were experimenting with many remarkable ideas, we youngsters enjoyed life as it was and found it good. We loved the winter and the dry snow. The streets were not cleared by ploughs, so the snow accumulated in high banks and the roadways mounted higher and higher. Sleighs were the only vehicles allowed because wheels would cut up the hard-packed snow and ruin the sledding, but children could have endless fun sliding down hills on sleds or toboggans and catching rides on low delivery sleighs. Some drivers allowed free riders but others yelled at us in French, and sometimes applied the horsewhip. Skis had not made their appearance so snowshoes were to be found in most houses. After a heavy storm I often snowshoed to school, and I wore moccasins all winter as being far superior to boots and rubbers.

The Mountain—that is, Mount Royal, from which the city gets its name—was the playground of the city. Unspoiled by traffic, it was a perfect park for anyone who wished to take advantage of it. Not everybody did, of course, but for the devotees of outdoor sports and exercise the mountain with its toboggan slides provided healthy and exciting sport.

Our home was only three blocks walk from the park of Mount Royal. With the exception of a main carriage drive, no attempt had been made to landscape the park and it was still in its natural wooded state. Its only buildings were the warden's residence on the north slope and a wooden look-out on the southeast side, from which, on a clear day, one could see most of the city and the great St. Lawrence River, the Lachine Rapids, St. Helen's Island and the Victoria Bridge, and a wide stretch of the Eastern Townships with their isolated mounts, clear through to the Green Mountains of Vermont. As a boy I walked over every inch of the park, except for the far northeastern side towards Fletcher's Field, which was regarded as French territory.

In those days squirrels were plentiful, mostly greys or reds, but on one never-to-be-forgotten day I spotted a pure white animal running along the top of a board fence. At first I thought it was a cat, but realized it was a squirrel when it was joined by another, equally white. They jumped to the ground inside the fence and ran to a big oak tree, which they climbed and entered, through a hole near the top of the trunk which was evidently their nest.

2

I had never before trespassed on this ground, which was surrounded by a board fence all along Pine Avenue and extended from opposite the tops of Simpson and Stanley Streets and northwards to the first park driveway, enclosing, I suppose, about eight or ten acres. This was virgin territory and I investigated every bit of it, dreaming of trapping the white squirrels alive in a big rat trap. The news was too good to keep so I took my best friend, Douglas Black, into my confidence. We smuggled a trap up the hill, disguised as lunch in a paper bag, and set it at the foot of the oak. But we caught nothing and to our great disappointment we never saw the white squirrels again. Somebody had been before us. However, this private lot became our happy hunting ground. Nobody ever came into the place. We felt like explorers in a new country.

A gurgling brook of pure, clear water ran from the crater of an extinct volcano on the mountaintop right through the property and was guided into a storm sewer at Pine Avenue. This provided our drinking water. We had never heard of pollution then; any clear water was supposed to be good, especially if it was running.

We discovered indisputable signs of an old house beside the brook. The house itself had long since been demolished and the debris carted away, but signs of a flagstone walk and very definite evidence of a garden were to be seen. Several species of perennial flowers and shrubs were plentiful. They were not wild, although the growth was ragged. The raspberries, gooseberries and black currants were of a variety we had never seen anywhere else on the mountain. I often wondered who built that house; it was most likely erected by someone who considered the slope of the mountain to be well out in the country at a time when Dorchester Street was uptown, and most of the large retail stores were on or near St. James Street.

Then there were dozens of outdoor rinks covered with natural ice. Boys and girls skated there, and our future hockey players learned their craft. Our home was on Lincoln Avenue, at that time one block long, not far from Guy Street on which the Patrick boys lived near Ste. Catherine. We boys enjoyed the privilege of flooding a small field in the orchard near where His Majesty's Theatre was later built. How did we get it flooded? Easy. Number 10 Fire Station was just around the corner on Ste. Catherine. Every day the beautiful black fire horses had to be taken out for an exercise run, so what was simpler than getting the firemen to hook up a length of hose to a nearby hydrant and flood the rink?

That's where the Patrick boys, Frank and Lester, later famous in international hockey, learned how to skate and stick-handle. They had a younger brother who had lost one leg as a small child, but he had as much spirit as his brothers and would show up with one skate on, a hockey stick in one hand and a crutch in the other, and proceed to mix it up with anybody.

Then there were toboggans. Nearly every child had a toboggan of some sort, even if it was only three feet long. Any hilly street provided a slide and Montreal is a city of hills. There was small danger from the traffic; that came later with the motor car, but then it took only moderate skill to avoid the slow-moving, horse-drawn sleighs.

In the days when Côte des Neiges (Hill of Snows) was almost entirely a country road between the big and little mountains, bobsleds were made by fastening a long plank to two ordinary sleds with steel runners. They were steered by the front man with a wheel. I was too young for this sport but Father told me how he and some friends would engage a cabman with one horse and a *berlot* (a low sleigh with wooden runners) to haul the bobsled to the top of the

Côte for twenty-five cents. (Incidentally, you could go anywhere in Montreal for twenty-five cents.)

With a little push the sled would start, gathering speed as it descended. Only a few *habitants* would be encountered slowly hauling their loads of manure home from the city's many stables. The sleds whizzed across Sherbrooke Street, down Guy and across Ste. Catherine, slowed a little before Dorchester and then plunged down the steep lower Guy Street hill, passed under the Canadian Pacific tracks and ended the run at the Grand Trunk (CNR) tracks. Another cabbie would be found and hired for one more run and that was all that could be accomplished in one afternoon.

The park slide on the north side of the mountain was very popular. A male had to pay one dollar for an annual membership, but ladies were carried free. This membership fee was imposed largely to limit the crowds of tobogganists who would have made the slide unmanageable. We were then given silk membership ribbons which we were required to sew on our blanket coats, just as the snowshoe-club members did. Our footwear consisted of moccasins, but the steersman usually wore a toecap made of rawhide to protect his moccasin from wearing through.

The park warden had erected a high platform, which we mounted by steps at the rear. From the top we could see many miles of the back country, which seemed to be all in farmland and forest. There before us were five or six iced chutes, built with wet snow which soon froze. A starter spaced the toboggans, for the heavier the load, the faster the toboggan would go. The riders did not sit up, but lay flat like shingles on a roof overlapping each other. The steersman sat on one hip so that he could swing his leg to steer. The speed was terrific and we would slide for about a quarter of a mile. After the last slide we would walk for a short distance out to Côte des Neiges and then slide all the way home, right to our front door on Lincoln Avenue. At that time there were very few buildings on the long hill now lined with tall apartment blocks and hospitals.

I used to feel sorry for those unfortunate boys who had to live in places like southern Ontario where they had cold weather but little snow.

Unlike today, when almost everybody owns a car, only the wealthy possessed horses and well-built stone stables in which to keep them. (Some of these stables were later turned into garages or even small homes.) The rest of the population walked to work or to church, school or theatre, unless they rode in the horsecars. (The horsecars, by the way, only went as far west as Guy Street, and then the horses were unhitched and driven around to the other end.) It was a treat for us when Father hired a cab twice a year, to carry us and our baggage between home and the station when we went on our summer holidays.

In winter, on Sunday afternoons, all the well-to-do gentry turned out and paraded back and forth behind their horses on Sherbrooke Street, which was a boulevard devoted to stone-built residences three storeys high and tastefully designed. The stone was usually white and was quarried near Montreal, with an occasional red sandstone. The builders were good Scottish masons for the most part. Nothing commercial was allowed on the street, which was one of the finest in North America. Many of the large homes were set well back from the street and surrounded by expensively built fences in stone and iron. Nowadays the profit motive has turned many of these fine homes into shops, or they have been demolished to make way for hotels and apartment blocks.

The beautifully groomed horses and splendidly equipped sleighs were hitched up in one of four styles: the modest equipages had one horse and others were drawn by a team; a third variation was called a unicorn, which consisted of a pair of horses with one in front; and a fourth, which looked quite Russian, was assembled as a troika—that is, with three horses abreast—but I never saw but one of those.

However the sleighs were harnessed, the occupants were invariably covered with fur robes while other robes hung from the back of the sleigh. If a coachman was employed he was dressed in a heavy fur cape, probably bearskin, and a huge busby-like fur cap.

The harnesses and shafts were liberally decorated with musical bells of various tones, and their jingling gave a gay carnival air to the whole spectacle. Hundreds of horses took part while thousands of Montrealers promenaded the sidewalks, many of them dressed in their best furs, men as well as women, their children clad in blanket coats, brightcoloured sashes and toques. The English preferred red while the French liked blue.

Snowshoers and tobogganists going to and from the mountain, all in their colourful costumes, added to a scene that was distinctly Canadian. All was peaceful and clean; there was no dirty slush, no traffic lights or cops, no bustle or hurry, no gas fumes or blaring horns.

No place in Canada, possibly in the world, could compare with it.

The clothing we wore, however, left much to be desired, especially in winter. In this field modern children's clothing is far superior. On the theory that weight made warmth and that wool was the best possible material for indoor or outdoor clothing, we were bundled into wool garments from head to foot. Of course, wool was good and warm, but it got wet easily. Even in the 1920s we were

7

still swathing our children in wool. As they came in from school or play, every stitch had to be removed and hung up to dry. We wore long woollen stockings that reached past our boots and above our knees. Compare this with the modern one-piece nylon winter coveralls, fastened with a zipper, removed in a jiffy, leaving everything dry underneath.

Even summer wear is much more comfortable, with its casual-looking shirts loose at the neck, and no hats. If I ever went out without a hat, Mother would call after me, "Come back here this instant and put on your cap. Do you want to get sunstroke?"

But of all the outrages perpetrated on the small boy, formal dress was the worst. The sailor suits weren't too bad with their starched collars hanging behind and with white bibs pinned in front. We even played games in these ridiculous outfits, unless, of course, it was a school match, and then we were permitted to wear jerseys. I longed for one of the new sweaters with a turtle-neck collar like the one our gymnastics master, Mr. Powter, wore, but Mother thought they were awful and wouldn't hear of it.

The worst "get up" of all was the Little Lord Fauntleroy suit. Somebody had published a book called *Little Lord Fauntleroy,* with illustrations, and it caught on. It showed this little sissy with *long curls* to the shoulder. The jacket was a short zouave affair with a lace collar to the shoulder seam, big pearl buttons and, so help me, a wide, black silk *sash* around the waist. A pair of short velvet pants and black patent-leather shoes completed the outfit. The women loved it and it was the ambition of every mother to trick out her darling in one of them and then display him in church or at parties. The unfortunate boy, of course, hoped that no one in his gang would see him.

About the time this folly was at its height, Mother's

brother (and my Uncle Horace) of Owen Sound, Ontario, decided to get married. Of course Father and Mother were invited. And *I* was supposed to go along because I was the only boy relative who possessed one of those absurd suits and could act as a flower girl or whatever. (Maybe it was a page.)

I suppose that I was what people used to call a "provoking child", for I flatly refused to wear the dress or to move a foot in the general direction of Georgian Bay. Mother was heartbroken and father was angry but I, to my everlasting credit, stood firm. Father issued an ultimatum: "Either you wear the suit or you stay at home."

They went without me.

What they did not realize, and I was too inarticulate to explain, was that if I had turned up in Owen Sound arrayed as planned, my life would not have been safe. I had no trouble imagining what would happen if I appeared before the tough, bare-footed gang of Huck Finns that hung around my cousin's corner. No, I couldn't face it. As Josh Billings once said, it would have been "2 mutch".

Another time Mother, whom I adored, brought home a pair of new shoes for me. Shoes at that time meant ankle-high boots and Mother thought they were very smart; but they were buttoned! Like a girl's! I would have done almost anything to please her, but not this. She couldn't understand me.

So if your child wants to wear white stockings when the script calls for black, why spoil a pleasant day making an issue of it? She will learn good taste soon enough. If she is out of line her friends will soon straighten her out or she will find out for herself.

Once a year Mother used to take me down to Henry Morgan's imposing department store (which still stands in the same location) to get fitted out with one of their famous sailor suits, which were almost a copy of those worn in the Royal Navy. The chief attraction of the suit for me was the free whistle on a white cord which was worn around the neck. On one of these occasions I stepped back to get a better view of myself in the long mirror when I felt something touch my shoulder, and then there was the sound of an awesome crash. I had backed into one of the magnificent four-foot-high porcelain jardinières, probably imported from China, that decorated the main floor. One glance told me that it was shattered beyond repair.

Mother was distraught and made haste to assure the salesman that she would, of course, pay for it. The salesman said that he would have to call Mr. Morgan himself and in a very short time the great man appeared, impressive in a frock coat and magnificent side whiskers. He merely cast a glance at the damage, told Mother not to worry and in the end she heard no more about it, which I thought was pretty generous treatment.

At the other end of the retail scale was Carsley's department store down on St. James Street in the midst of the financial district, as other stores such as Birks were at that time. Everything was cheap at Carsley's and at Christmas it was an overheated madhouse. There were no cash registers in those days, so when a customer paid the bill, the salesgirl hauled down by a piece of rope a small metal container, put the sales slip and the cash inside, let it go up and then jerked the rope, and the box went whizzing to the main cash desk. This system would not, however, stand up to the Christmas rush, so a gaggle of little boys and girls was hired. A customer handed over a bank note, the girl screamed CASH at the top of her voice, because she had to compete with fifty others, and presently a small urchin would appear. The salesgirl would give him the money and off he would scoot. If he could remember where he got it, he returned with the change.

What with the crowds, and the heat in our winter clothing, the melted snow on the floor and the yelling for CASH, Carsley's at Christmas was bedlam. But we continued to go, for at that time Carsley's was the only store in town that had a Santa Claus, and we kids thought that he was the original, living St. Nicholas.

Mr. Carsley had a lovely home on Guy Street opposite the end of Lincoln Avenue. It was surrounded by at least an acre of grounds and bordered with shady trees. A high board fence kept out the curious and there was a large gate for guests with their horses and carriages. On the Queen's birthday, the 24th of May, Carsley gave his cash-boys and girls a magnificent party. They stuffed themselves with cake and ice cream and popcorn, and then, when it began to get dark, there was always an enormous fireworks display which was the signal that the party was over.

Father was a great snowshoer and one of the founders of the St. George Snowshoe Club, whose clubhouse still stands on the Little Mountain in upper Westmount but is now used for other purposes. (In my youth, that area was known as Côte St. Antoine, and was an area of orchards.) He taught me how to walk on snowshoes at a very early age, probably at about five or six years, and showed me how to tie a Hudson's Bay hitch with either deerhide thongs or with lamp wick.

He also used to see to it that his father, an ex-factor with the Hudson's Bay Company at Fort William, kept me well supplied with Indian-made deerskin moccasins. All of our playmates wore factory-made imitations of the Indian article, equipped with metal eyelets and laces. But Father classified all factory-made moccasins as "Niagara Falls trash". The Indian product had a thick but soft hide. The tops were two flaps, tied together with deerskin thongs. The toe pieces were always cleverly embroidered with multi-coloured beads or dyed porcupine quills, or perhaps they were tastefully stitched with silk thread. When they dried out after a wetting in slushy snow they got hard, but a vigorous rubbing soon restored their former softness.

All the snowshoe clubs went on long tramps at the weekend, sometimes as far as Lachine, and all the members were attired in blanket suits of their club colours. The members of St. George's wore a thigh-length coat and white knee-length pants with purple stripes. Toque, sash and stockings were purple.

When I was about nine years old, Father took me on one of their tramps. We assembled on Dominion Square, facing Windsor Hotel, and there snowshoes were tied on. The club then snowshoed up the steep, upper Peel Street hill to Pine Avenue, where the Mountain Park began. We climbed over the Mountain and down the other side, into the open country. Then we swung to the left, crossed Côte des Neiges at its summit and circled around the back of the Little Mountain, down the south slope to the clubhouse. Towards the end I could hardly keep up, but I was determined to finish on my own feet so two good-natured members dropped back to keep me company and I reached the club standing up.

After five years of snowshoeing and tobogganing, my introduction to skiing came about in a rather curious manner during the winter of 1898-99.

At that time I was a student at the Montreal High School and had formed a friendship with Eric McQuaig (who was to become a brigadier general in the First World War). Eric's elder brother had some connection with the Finland Navigation Company and on returning from one of his trips to Finland had brought with him a pair of skis.

He hung them on the wall of his bedroom as trophies, like a pair of swords.

Of course we had read about skis in the *Boy's Own Annual* and we knew that they were used in Scandinavian countries, but they did not cause any more excitement than the knowledge that Spaniards held bullfights. They were just something different and foreign that we had never seen before.

They were about six feet long, broader than later models, and had a groove on the underside. The binding was of the most primitive kind; it consisted of one broad leather strap to keep the foot from falling out. The Finns wore a high boot of soft leather with a turned-up curlicue toe which was hooked through the strap. Only one pole came with the skis; it was a stout wooden staff something like a broomstick, which was forced through a thick, circular leather disc which served the same purpose as the lightweight basket-like ring that is used today.

The Scandinavians used their skis as a means of transportation when travelling or hunting and not for sport, in the same way as our Canadian Indians used snowshoes. If they had to run down a hill they simply pointed their toes downwards and let go in a straight line. There was none of this serpentining down slopes in a series of connected turns that the moderns use. To stop, they braked hard by leaning on the pole, and if that did not bring them to a halt then they simply sat down in the snow.

Much later the Norwegians developed a turn and called it the telemark, after a hill in their own country. This was a long, graceful, sweeping turn which brought the weight of the body to either side by bending one knee until it nearly touched the ski. This turn was made possible because of the one-strap fitting; it would be impossible with the rigid modern binding which clamps the ski to the boot like a skate.

In the course of time Englishmen, visiting Norway, realized the possibilities of the ski for sport. With the English genius for organizing games, they took it to Switzerland where they had been mountain climbing for years, and developed the beginnings of modern skiing.

Eric and I purchased his brother's skis for $2.50 on a partnership basis and took them up on the mountain as soon as we had a chance. We knew absolutely nothing about their use and there were no instructors or books that might have helped us to learn. We just decided to treat them as two narrow twin toboggans. One simply pointed them downhill and shoved off, aided by a push from the pole. Once the skis came to a stop, the rider removed them and carried them back uphill where he handed them over to his waiting partner.

On the way home, people stopped us and asked, "What are those things?"

It is a fact that in that year, no store selling sporting goods offered a pair for sale. Some had heard of them; others had not. I never saw another pair in Montreal before I left that city in 1902. I think it is fair to say that Eric and I, if not the first, were certainly among the very earliest to use skis in Montreal.

In the spring I bought out Eric's share as he had decided to make a pair for himself. Unfortunately, I broke one of mine from end to end one day, coming down Peel Street, by striking a stone of macadamized roadway that had worked up to the surface through the snow.

When I returned to Canada in 1919 after the war, skiing was becoming popular, but even so one could not buy any proper ski clothing in Toronto. One store urged me to buy a pair of knee-high, RCMP boots as the proper apparel for skiing. No skis were being made in Canada and the pair I bought were manufactured in Minneapolis.

On one of his rare visits to Montreal, my grandfather, the old Scot from Fort William who called his house there Glenorchy, stayed with us. He was not tall but, like most highlanders, he was very sturdily built; a French Canadian once described him as "not very high but tall across". He grew his white whiskers from ear to ear, looked very stern and had little to say, and he had no time at all for children, whom he thought should be seen and not heard. Secretly I was afraid of him, but Father was justly proud of the old man, who had a wonderful record of service in the northern wilderness.

He had travelled around the world, across Siberia and Russia on horseback, with Sir George Simpson, governor of the Hudson's Bay Company.

It was arranged that we should be photographed together—the three generations. Just a little memento for posterity.

The plan was that Father would wait downtown at Notman's while I hurried home from school, changed my clothes and then went with Grand-dad to meet Dad.

Boy-like, when school was out, I forgot all about it and became involved in a snowball fight in which I got well mussed up. Suddenly I remembered the appointment. I ran all of the seven blocks home to Guy Street where I collided with Grand-dad coming around a corner, looking very grim. He collared me in a no-nonsense grip and, in spite of my protests that I must go home and change into my sailor suit, he said, "We have no time. Come with me."

Now I was in deep trouble. Both Father and the old Scot would be annoyed because I was late and Mother would be worrying because I had not come home. She did indeed phone the police, thinking that I might be lost or, even worse, that I had reached Notman's improperly dressed.

When the photographer began to arrange his subjects

it was discovered that my left stocking had a gaping hole in the knee. As Mr. Notman could not supply another pair of hose, it was decided as an emergency measure that Grand-dad would be seated as befitted his dignity, Father would stand behind his chair (I could not stand there to hide the stocking because nothing would be seen of me but the hair on top of my head), and I would stand in front with my legs crossed to hide the hole. I was wearing my school out-door reefer with one brass button missing, but it was neces-sary to hide a rather dishevelled blouse underneath.

Father was a man of many parts but with no regular income. His business was railway supplies and when business was good, we lived high. But when it was below par, Mother was forced to adopt all sorts of economies. In a prosperous year Father would send all the family to the seaside in Maine for the whole summer and we would live well at a hotel. One year he treated himself to a winter in Italy and brought back a trunk full of beautiful silks and lace as well as Venetian glassware, ornaments, cameos and jewellery.

In our depressed periods, when Mother had to scrimp, conditions were more difficult for her than any of us. One Saturday she took me to the Mountain Street Market at the foot of the hill near St. Antoine in order to help her carry the purchases home. I was fascinated with the market because it had a great variety of live animals and birds for sale, on the hoof as it were. There were puppies and rabbits, guinea pigs and white rats and mice, chickens and ducks and pigeons.

She shopped carefully and I still remember some of the items. A pair of chickens, plucked but not drawn, at 35 cents a pair. (I think that if she had complained a little more vigorously and in a louder voice they might have thrown in another.) One huge cauliflower at 5 cents, two dozen oysters right off one of the oyster boats from Prince Edward Island, and a whole mess of vegetables and fruit. Anyway, we filled up two market baskets and started up the steep hill on foot. On the way, while we paused for breath, she said, "Your Uncle Henry is coming for a visit tomorrow. Now, I like Henry and I want to entertain him well because he doesn't come often, but this dinner is going to cost me a dollar." She cooked it herself and all five of us enjoyed it.

I attended the Montreal High School when it was on Peel Street where the Mount Royal Hotel stands now. I liked the school and all the teachers but one. Contrary to what some people believe, boys like a strict teacher so long as he or she is fair; then they know where they stand. My favourite was Mr. Isaac Gemmel who taught history, including scripture history, and geography. Scripture was not taught as a religious subject but as straight history. Mr. Gemmel implanted in my mind a love of those subjects that has never left me. He made the leading characters in history, from Abraham to the heroes of Queen Victoria's time, stand out as real people. The geography book came to life under his hands too. He was not so much interested in the population of Peru or the products of the Congo as he was in the physical features of those countries, and the people. He made us look at their countries as places we all wanted to visit some day.

He was a remarkable man. Many years after I had left school, I found myself in Montreal on business. I looked up and saw a street sign: "University St." This was the street where the new high school was located, up near McGill University. I decided that I would pay it a visit. I was now forty years old but, never mind, I would go in and look at the Memorial Tablet that had been erected to the young men of the high school who had volunteered their services in the First World War. There it was in the entrance hall. I looked at the names, many of them familiar, and why not? These were my schoolmates. This was the generation that had fought the war. Just grown-up schoolboys. Eleven hundred and thirty-one who volunteered to fight for their country. They would have made a battalion at full strength if they could have been gathered together.

One hundred and fifty-four are buried overseas. May their names live forever more.

How the faces and names came flooding back, many from old and well-known Montreal families, and many in groups of two or three brothers.

Footsteps sounded in the corridor. It was the janitor.

"Who is the principal of this school now?" I asked.

"Mr. Gemmel, sir."

"Is he in?"

"Yes, sir. That's his room right there. Just knock and go right in."

I entered and there was old Gammalial, as we fondly used to call him.

I had left this school in 1900, twenty-five years before, a boy in short pants and probably needing a haircut. Now I was a man grown, with a mustache and thinning hair. A father, no less, with children. An ex-colonel in the army. He must have met and taught at least 2,500 boys since he last saw me. I advanced towards his desk.

"I don't suppose you remember me, Mr. Gemmel," was my opening remark.

"Of course I remember you, Macintyre," was his astonishing reply as he rose to shake hands.

Such a feat of memory amazed me. No wonder we loved him.

18

I reluctantly left school in 1900 and went to work the next day in the real-estate office of J. Cradock Simpson and Co., as an office boy.

The hours were long and the pay was small. Every Saturday the old bookkeeper, Mr. Sears, an Indian Mutiny veteran with side whiskers, dug into his cash box and gave me three dollars. I lived at home but I had to buy all my own clothes, streetcar fare and lunches. A light lunch cost about fifteen cents and car tickets were six for a quarter. As I had not graduated from school I thought that I should get some more education, so I took French and shorthand at the YMCA and drawing at the Monument Nationale on St. Lawrence Street. The latter was a long walk from Lincoln Avenue, after a day's work; however I enjoyed the sketching and did two years' work in one.

I spent two years at Cradock Simpson's that were notable for nothing so much as the difference in the office routine of that time as compared to the present. We had one typewriter which was operated from time to time by a junior male clerk named Hugh Millar, but the chief's son Percy and the insurance clerk, Jackson, kept agitating for a full-time stenographer-typist. Women at that time were rarely seen in offices. The Old Man thought that a woman's presence would demoralize the staff, but finally broke down and an attractive young French *Canadienne* was engaged. She bore an old French name, Antoinette de Rouville, and must have come from a good family. She was competent and bilingual and was soon a favourite with everyone.

My desk was next to hers and I was so shy that I could hardly speak to her. However, she was very kind to a bashful boy and I would have done anything I could to help her.

The Old Man wrote all his letters by hand, even after Antoinette came. He used an old-fashioned steel pen which he dipped into a bottle of special purple copying ink.

We used no carbon paper in the office, so that all letters and invoices had to be copied by the wet press method, which was efficient enough but slow and messy. Nobody under sixty is likely ever to have seen one of these contraptions, so I shall describe it briefly.

The copying was done at a long table near the walk-in vault. On the table a heavy metal press was set up. This press was equipped with a horizontal wheel for holding the copy book steady. All the pages in the book were numbered to make indexing easy. At the first blank page, a sheet of stiff, oiled paper was inserted and covered by the tissue page which was then swabbed over lightly with a wet whitewash brush kept in a water can. This is where the office boy could get into trouble, for if the page was too wet the ink would be blurred, and if it was not damp enough, it would make a poor copy. Having placed the letter in the book on top of the wet page, the big screw was twisted down tightly on the book and held there for a minute, then released, and the letter, or letters, removed and spread out to dry. Hence the need of a long table. I often did a dozen at once.

Mr. Simpson was the grandson of a full-blooded Indian chief from the Penetanguishene area, but the only distinguishing mark he displayed was his long stride with his toes turned in. He was a very fine old gentleman, well educated and well read. In fact, his home library was a treasure house to me when I went over there to play with Alan.

Because Mr. Simpson had a deep distrust of the ordinary street letterbox, I had to collect all of our mail at a box in the Montreal General Post Office on St. James Street and in the evening take all the outgoing mail there. Since he registered many of his letters, I had to wait in line, and since there were many boys like me it was often seven o'clock when I got home.

Mr. Simpson had several very important clients whose property he managed. One was Lord Strathcona and Mount Royal, a multi-millionaire and a director of the CPR, the man who had driven the last spike in the railway in 1885. He had a modest office near ours. I used to be sent over there with letters to deliver as I was considered to be more reliable than the post office. Old Mr. Hardisty, who had been with Strathcona for years in the Hudson's Bay Company, was all the staff he seemed to have, but sometimes the door to his private office would be open and I could see the great man sitting at his desk, his white beard and his enormous white eyebrows jutting straight out an inch and a half from his brow, making him easy to recognize. Those eyebrows were the delight of the cartoonists of the day. I have in my possession a number of letters Strathcona wrote to my grandfather when he was plain Donald Smith of the Hudson's Bay Co. and John McIntyre was a factor at Fort William, but I did not have the nerve to walk in and tell him who I was.

During all this period in a Montreal office, the British were fighting a war with the hardy Boer farmers and ranchers in South Africa. Canada sent several thousand volunteers, and Percy Simpson and Jackson were among them. They came down to say good-bye in uniform and we were very proud of them.

The French Canadians did not approve of the war and campaigned actively against it in the press and with meetings and parades. These street demonstrations often led to fights. I was present when the McGill students attacked Laval University when it was on St. Denis Street. It was a terrible night and we were in the grip of one of the worst snowstorms in Montreal's history. It snowed and drifted for three days and many streets had to be closed. The university buildings were in darkness. The students tried the big doors, but found them locked. Then they forced their way in and were greeted by streams of ice-cold water from the fire hoses in the lobby. This cooled them off and they stamped around clanking with ice. Laval retaliated by a mass march on McGill a few nights later. They were reinforced by workmen from the Mont St. Louis quarries carrying sledgehammers. McGill scouts on horseback brought back news of their approach, but they never reached the gates because French-speaking police stopped them short of their objective.

There were many street brawls. The French tore down the big news bulletins in front of the Montreal Star building when Ladysmith in South Africa, which had been under seige for a long time, was relieved. The English-speaking part of Montreal celebrated with parades and flags. They marched on City Hall and demanded that the Union Jack be flown from the tower. This the Mayor did, under protest. On the way back, when the crowd noticed that the anti-British paper *La Patrie* was not flying the flag, they broke in and wrecked some of the machinery. These incidents and many others demonstrate the depth of feeling that prevailed. It was dangerous for an English-speaking person to go east of Bleury on Ste. Catherine wearing a patriotic button of any kind for fear of a beating. Space does not permit me to record much of what happened, but the seeds of discord sown then were reaped in 1914-18.

The French regarded the war as an imperialistic struggle deliberately provoked by Britain to grab the rich gold mines of the Transvaal. We thought it our duty to support Britain, but the French would have no part in any foreign war.

Looking back on events after the passage of many years, and the reading of much history, I am inclined to think that the French were right in their opinion but wrong to oppose our country's effort by force and propaganda. Our course was to be loyal to Britain, the mother country of most of Canada's citizens.

Our office was located in a semi-basement with a large plate-glass window facing St. James Street. At the rear were the offices of the Dominion Burglary Alarm Co.

One winter night when we were working late (as usual), fire broke out in the rear office. The lights went out in a few minutes and there was much confusion. Old Mr. Sears wanted to save his books and cash boxes, of which he had several, one for each estate. It was not sufficient, in his opinion, to keep the estate accounts separate in the books—the actual cash was kept separate in different boxes. Antoinette was calling, "Where are my rubbers?" Everyone was telling me to get things into the vault. When everybody but me was out I looked about and saw by the light of a street lamp a cash box that had been overlooked. But by then somebody had closed the vault door. The flames and smoke were getting pretty close, so I ran out with the cash box just as the fire brigade broke the plate-glass window so that they could flood the office. The street crowd was small at that time of night, but I could see no member of our staff so I was stuck with the cash. I considered carrying it home but was afraid to, in case some thief might snatch it and run, so I went down to the old *Daily Witness* office on Craig Street where I could see a light in the window. I found a bookkeeper working late. I persuaded him, much against his will, to keep the box in his vault for the night. Next morning our old office and everything in it was sheathed in ice three or four inches thick.

The horses of the Montreal Fire Department were usually

Percherons and the best money could buy. Big, strong, beautiful animals and always jet black.

I have already said that I lived near No. 10 station, so I often saw the brigade turn out.

When an alarm came in to the station, the horses recognized it and fidgeted to go. They lived in box stalls and were left loose. When a fireman opened the stall door each horse trotted quickly to his place. As soon as he was in position, a complete set of harness was lowered from the ceiling on to his back. It remained only to couple his heavy collar, snap it shut and buckle a few straps, and he was ready. It took no more than a minute . . . less time than warming up a motor. The firemen on duty came running or sliding down a brass pole to their vehicles. If they had been sleeping, they pulled their clothes on as they ran.

The big front doors were swung upward and the horses dashed out at full speed. There were no traffic lights or traffic cops in those days. The big brass bell on each machine was rung continuously by one of the crew. Everybody had learned to keep well out of the way.

To see the "reels" go by was a sight never to be forgotten. The horses knew they were going to a fire, and with stretched-out legs, raced at full gallop. They had the middle of the street to themselves. Sparks flew from their flying feet as they struck the cobblestones.

We of the Lincoln Avenue gang were sure that No. 10 was always first at every fire, no matter where it was.

When electric streetcars were first introduced in Montreal, the company ordered a sort of fishnet attached to a U-shaped iron bar to be hung on the front of the car. The idea was that if some unwary citizen fell flat on his face on the track in front of a moving car, the motorman could press a hand lever and scoop him up neatly like a trout. This device

24

was planned to save the pedestrian from injury and the company from law suits. However, after a trial period the company decided that the attachment was unnecessary as nobody had been obliging enough to test it by falling down at the right time and place.

Another odd practice was used in transferring passengers at a street junction. For instance, if a Ste. Catherine Street car heading west had twelve passengers who wanted to transfer to a Windsor car going south, the conductor would herd his dozen on the corner and wait for the Windsor car. When it arrived he would shout to his opposite number, "Douze", and his customers would walk across and be counted in. Trouble arose when some unscrupulous ringer would join in the parade about the middle and would be counted "in" with the others, making the score thirteen. An argument would arise when the innocent thirteenth man attempted to board, an argument that the conductor couldn't win against all the other witnesses talking at once. Under those circumstances the company was forced to issue printed transfers.

In 1901 and 1902 Montreal was devastated by a four-pronged plague, an event that influenced my future life. The city was not prepared for it and the Isolation Hospital on Fletcher's Field was soon overcrowded. Four different diseases struck the city at the same time and in the depth of winter. The great killer was scarlet fever, closely followed by diphtheria, typhoid fever and smallpox. During the two winters that the epidemic raged, no less than 6,328 persons were quarantined and 1,160 died.

Today the health department of any modern city would consider itself disgraced to have even one case of typhoid, as it would reflect on its control of the water and milk supply, but in the early days of this century health control of infectious and contagious diseases left much to be desired. They did their best with what knowledge and preventatives they had, but there was much to be learned and applied.

At any rate, I came down with a severe case of scarlet fever. Mother phoned eight doctors before she could get one overworked physician to come and look at me. It was just as well that I could not get into the isolation hospital as it was already overcrowded and a patient who was sent there with scarlet fever might well die of diphtheria or smallpox.

Getting a nurse was out of the question since every nurse in the city was already working overtime, so there was nothing for it but to be quarantined in our flat on Stanley Street and install Mother as nurse. Father and Pearl had to pack up and leave that night. Rooms were found not far away. A sheet soaked in disinfectant was hung over the front door and a sign with the word SCARLETINA in red tacked up. For six weeks I lay in bed while Mother never once left the house. I was not allowed up until all the skin on my body had peeled off.

2 THE SURVEY PARTY

As I lay with little to do, I thought about my future. I decided that the first thing to be done was to regain my health and build up my body. To do this I must have plenty of fresh air and exercise, and this could only be obtained by living in the country. I thought that life on a survey party would be just the thing so I sought Father's advice. He suggested that I write to the chief engineer of the CPR and ask about a job as chain man on one of the many survey parties going out that spring. I followed his advice and in a few days received a letter from Mr. W.F. Tye, chief engineer, saying that he might find a place for me but that I must apply formally and state my weight and height. Apparently the company was not interested in my educational qualifications nor in my character; their attitude was that it was a rugged life and I had to be tough to last out the summer. I was accepted soon after I sent in my application and told to report to Mr. G.H. Garden, the engineer in charge of the party, at Place Viger Station at 5 p.m. on the 21st of April, 1902.

As soon as I could walk about, I began to acquire an outfit of clothing suitable for the Quebec bush. I favoured corduroy for the breeches and it proved to be a good choice. My shirts were of flannel, one grey and one navy blue. Socks had to be long and of heavy wool, but the most important item of all was footwear, for we would be walking many miles a day. My choice was for the long *bottes sauvages* (wilderness boots) that the French habitants wore. They were knee-length, soft leather boots without any soles or heels, something like Eskimo mukluks. No laces were required but a strap ran through two loops at the top of the knee to hold them up. They had the advantage of being serviceable in summer or winter, as they were warm and waterproof and, worn with two pairs of lumberman's socks, they were very comfortable. They were also very cheap, since every village cobbler could make them.

The great day came and I went down to meet the party at the station. Mr. Garden was a New Brunswicker and an old surveyor. I soon found out that he knew his trade, but suffered from diabetes which made the poor man short tempered. Officially he was the assistant engineer, but we came to call him "Almighty Voice". His nephew, Ben Copeland, was the transit man and second in command. The rod man was Bill Lewis, an old mounted policeman. Fred

Rutter, a University of Toronto student and I were the chain men. Later we picked up two expert axe men at Labelle, our destination, one hundred miles north of Montreal in the Laurentian hills.

On the trip up from Montreal, a fussy French-speaking woman boarded the train at St. Jerome with her arms full of parcels. Our conductor on this occasion was a large, important looking official, resplendent in his spotless blue uniform with brass buttons gleaming. He came through the car to collect Madame's ticket and she asked him if the train was on time.

"No, Madame," he replied gravely. "It is five minutes late."

The conductor was evidently well known to the passengers, and later I got to know him and three or four of his brothers, all conductors or trainmen. Their name was Latour.

From then on, as we wound our way through the beautiful Laurentian Hills, she would pester him with questions about the train's progress. Finally he drew himself up and, holding out his massive gold watch, he announced so that all might hear:

"Madame, we are due at Labelle at 10 p.m. We are now twenty minutes late. If you have been well educated, calculate that."

The crowd loved it and shouted its approval—all of this in French, of course, which made it sound better.

We arrived at Labelle about 10 p.m. and were taken to the Hotel du Nord.

The personnel of the party changed as summer slipped into fall. To keep the record straight, Mr. Garden was replaced by Mr. C.A. Mitchell; Copeland was transferred and a Yankee named Waterman, a graduate of Boston Tech, replaced him; Lewis left and was replaced by "Klondike"

Bill Rosamund of Almonte, Ontario; another American, Harry Ruhl from Pennsylvania, took Rutter's place; and Perley from New Brunswick joined the crew.

"Klondike" was a character who had been so named because he had taken part in the Klondike gold rush. He was the son of well-to-do parents and could afford to dress well, but he was curiously indifferent about his clothing. When reproached for his lack of neatness, he said, "What's the difference how I look? Up here in the bush nobody knows me, and back home everybody knows me, so what's the point of dressing up to impress them?"

The morning after our arrival the axe men reported. One was Napoleon Paquin, an elderly man with grey hair, rather slight of build but an artist at his craft as I soon found out. The other was Joe Tetley, a burly younger man who had learned his job as a lumberjack and homesteader. As the job included board, he had walked six miles so as to get a free breakfast. I always admire a man who is good at his craft, whether he be an axe man or a surgeon, and as these men were with us all summer I grew to like and respect them. Ever since then I have enjoyed working with a good sharp axe.

Perhaps it would help if I explained the reasons for this expedition.

Twenty miles north of Labelle lay new country with few farms; that is, much of it was still government land and was open for homesteading. It was all forest land, and lumber companies had been taking mostly pine out of it for years. Now the Quebec government was anxious to fill it with settlers, just as the Dominion government was filling the West with settlers, but with this difference: in the West, a man from any nation or any part of Canada could file on 160 acres of free land, but in Quebec the provincial government wanted only its own people from the older settled districts and ex-Canadians from the New England states. These were sure to be almost entirely French-speaking settlers. In this way the government of Quebec kept its own people at home and ensured the preservation of their language and religion. The bait was one hundred acres of free land.

In order to provide transportation for the people of Quebec who wished to settle in the Laurentian hills north of Montreal, a line called the Montreal and Western was built as far as Labelle, one hundred miles distant. This line was leased to the Canadian Pacific Railway in 1890, and in 1897 was purchased by that company and called the Labelle branch.

In 1899 a new company called *Le chemin de fer de colonisation du Nord* (Northern Colonization Railway), with Senator J.B. Rolland as its president, was formed for the purpose of extending the line from Labelle to Mont Laurier. However, this new company never built or operated one yard of the line. In 1902 the CPR, from its northern terminus at Labelle and on an understanding with the NCR, began the construction of the twenty-one mile extension to Lake Nominingue, which was completed in 1904 when the CPR leased it from the NCR for a period of 999 years; in other words, in perpetuity. The line was again extended to its present terminus at Mont Laurier a few years later.

It was during these two years of construction that I worked for the CPR in Quebec.

The Canadian Pacific was the first railway to span Canada from coast to coast. Without that railway we could not have developed the western provinces into a productive region. It became, in a short time, the backbone of the Dominion, linking all the regions of Canada together.

The task of spanning the continent was completed in record time, despite the difficult terrain encountered along the north shore of Lake Superior and in the Rocky Mountains. But the railway-builders were immediately faced with the necessity of building branch lines in all directions, especially in the three prairie provinces of Manitoba, Saskatchewan and Alberta, where settlers were rapidly filling up the country and needed an outlet for their grain.

For some reason unknown to me the last section of the Labelle branch had been carried three miles beyond Labelle and ended in the bush. There it lay, its rails rusted, its wooden culverts fallen in, some of its fences lying on the ground. Here and there a piece of the grade had washed away. Small trees had grown between the rails. This was the end of steel.

Some time before, a trial or reconnaissance line had been surveyed by an engineer named Lumsden. The purpose of such a line was to determine in a rough fashion where the new line was to be built and approximately what it might cost. Sometimes several of these trial lines would be run. We found the stakes marked with an L.

Now the company had made a decision to extend the line to beautiful little Lac Nominingue and its village, twenty-one miles to the northwest, and Mr. Garden's task was to locate the route definitely. This was called a location survey. On such a survey, accurate measurements would be taken to an inch; the levels of the surrounding land with all its contours would be measured and the position of streams, lakes, swamps and rock escarpments located accurately. Location was usually followed by construction, but not necessarily at once.

Mr. Garden was familiar with this country, which was populated entirely by French Canadians as far as settlement reached. Few people knew any English, so a working knowledge of French was necessary. Mr. Garden, Ben Copeland and I all had enough French to get along with the people;

in fact, I saw it as a first-class chance to improve my limited French and I have been thankful for it all my life. There was some risk in trying to learn pure French by this method because the people still talked with the accent of Old Normandy. Fortunately I had learned enough Parisian French in school to be able to detect the difference. A common example was the local habit of pronouncing "oui" like "way" instead of like "wee", and "toi" like "tway".

There is nothing unusual about this in any language. It does not mean ignorance but hundreds of years of local custom. The English are a good example: their pronunciation varies from county to county, so that a Yorkshireman and a London cockney can hardly understand each other. Who is to say which is right? For my money, the English spoken by the ladies of Edinburgh is the most pleasant of all.

The morning after our arrival Mr. Gordon hired a team and a light wagon with a driver, and we all went out to the end of track, unloaded our instruments and our lunch and went to work. The first thing that the chief did was to locate the exact end of steel, which he did by finding a thick plug of wood, called a hub, in the centre of the old track. Copeland set up his transit on its three legs and got a sight ahead. Fred carried the hundred-foot chain forward while I held the other end to the hub. The chain we used was made of one hundred one-foot links with brass tabs at ten-foot intervals. Fred also had a picket about six feet long painted red and white, with a steel point. He was waved into position by the transit man; the chain was pulled taut, and then the picket was pushed in at the right spot. Surveyors call this hundred-foot length a "station", and a freshly cut wooden stake was driven in and checked again by Ben. If the line changed direction before the next station, the distance would be measured and the stake marked in blue lumber crayon. Taking the first station as number one, then the next stake at a change of direction, say fifty-seven feet beyond that, would be marked 1.57 and so on, to the end of the survey. From then on all the references to locations would be designated by these station numbers and contracts would be made by them. A small contractor with maybe one or two teams of horses might build one or two stations in favourable soil that he could handle, and he was called a "station man". Large contractors might let out a considerable part of their section to smaller contractors.

As we proceeded, the axe men felled all trees and cleared all brush out of the way for the transit man. If the bush was heavy more axe men would be hired, farm youths used to the work. Since we could not proceed until the line was clear, Fred and I would help as well as we could. My experience with an axe had been limited to chopping ice off the sidewalk at home and I doubt that Fred had even that much, but the two of us would worry away at a tree until it fell. Our stumps always looked as though the trees had been chewed down by beavers while, with far less sweat, Paquin would fell his tree just where he wanted it and leave a stump that looked as though it had been planed.

The professional axe men, I noticed, always kept their axes sharp as razors, working every night with the aid of the farmer's grindstone and finishing off with their own whetstone.

The pioneer of the backwoods is seldom far from his axe and is so accustomed to the feel of an axe handle that he frequently uses the tool for other purposes than felling trees. If Paquin broke or blunted his pencil, he would sharpen it with his axe. He also used it, naturally, to open a can of tomatoes or as a hammer or a sledge. In climbing up steep, pathless hills, he hooked it around a sapling above his head to pull himself up. Of course, all of the stakes and hubs were made with the axe.

34

Paquin taught me a useful little lesson one day. We were working through country that had been burned off some time previously and was now covered with fallen and standing trees burned black. This kind of region was called *brulé*, and from walking through it, climbing over big fallen trees and cutting wood for stakes, we got very dirty. The mosquitoes were troublesome in the spring and, in slapping them off our faces, we became blackfaced too. The small saplings I was accustomed to use for making stakes were hard to find and I was complaining about this to Paquin. He smiled, and taking his sharp axe he walked over to a large fallen pine, shoulder high as it lay on the ground, in which he cut two notches on the side. Then he cut downwards and with a quick flip of his wrist stripped off piece after piece about two feet long and straight as a ruler. In this way he soon had a little pile of straight pine slabs which he smoothed at one end and pointed at the other. There is no wood more pleasant to work with than pine, it is so white and straight grained and its shavings so like silk.

At noon there was a halt for lunch, which was invariably the same thing as the day before. The lunch was packed in a pail and carried up to us by one of the party. In a little cleared space a fire would be lit, and two forked green sticks would be driven into the ground with another green stick laid across. On this the pailful of water would be hung, and when the water had boiled a handful of green tea would be thrown in. The rest of the lunch consisted of a loaf of bread hollowed out in the centre to hold a lump of butter, and several cans of stewed tomatoes, which we drank straight out of the can, opened by two slashes of a hatchet, or out of tin pannikins supplied for cups.

We never deviated from the line no matter what the terrain was like; we just took the country as it came. If the line ran through muskeg or across a creek, we waded through it, and if our boots took in too much water we emptied them out on the other side. Generally speaking, our feet were always wet.

At the day's end, around six o'clock, we made for the nearest road and followed it home, hoping to meet the team on the way. If there was no road then we simply followed our own trail back to our starting place. At the beginning we would walk about ten miles a day, but as the line was pushed farther on the walks became longer and would often run to twenty miles a day. When it extended that far we would have to move camp farther ahead and work back and forth.

The worst billet on the line was a farmhouse on the opposite side of the river from Vilani's sawmill. It was a small log building that had been insulated against the winter cold by plastering all the inside walls with cow manure mixed with straw. No doubt it would be warm in winter, but in July's heat the atmosphere in a bedroom where four men slept with windows nailed shut can be imagined.

The incident that I remember best about that home occurred one day when mail arrived in our absence, including a bundle of illustrated magazines from my father. The youngest child in the family, knowing no better, opened the parcel, took all the magazines out and, without any interference from her mother, tore out all the pictures and spread them on the floor for her amusement. To say the least I was annoyed, not with the child but with her careless mother.

The eldest son, a sturdy lad who worked with us as an axe man, bore the proud name of Clovis after the famous hero knight who became King of France in the early years of the sixth century.

My most pleasant memory of that spot is of the nearby riverbank where I used to sit in the spring evenings and watch the swiftly flowing river, which seemed to be gathering its strength for the plunge down the Twin Sisters Rapids.

At that time of the day the Wilson thrush poured out its beautiful song in a cascade of melody which I long to hear again, but never shall.

It was near this place that I nearly lost my life. We were working on the east side of the river, running a trial line and using a narrow farm track cut into the side hill and bordered by a rail fence on the riverside. From the track to the river was a drop of about fifteen feet. Our line crossed the fence at a narrow angle and went down the hill to the riverbank. I was head chain man and was pulling the chain with my left hand, which also held an axe. In my right arm I held a bundle of stakes, so my hands were fully occupied and of no use to me in crossing the fence. I sat on the fence's top rail with my back to the river and swung my legs over, but at the start of the swing the top rail snapped in two with a sharp crack. I fell backward, and all that I can remember is that one instant I could see the blue sky and the next I was looking at the ground apparently rushing up to meet me. I clearly saw an old stump and figured that it would break my back if I hit it, but luckily I landed beside it on the sandy shore.

I lay there winded and looked up at my comrades peering down on me in alarm. In a few moments I caught my breath, got to my feet and climbed up with some help at the top from members of the party.

That was the first and only time I ever heard Mr. Garden, who was usually pretty gruff, express any sentiment.

"If you had hit that stump lad, I would have had to go home around some other way."

In a short time we came to the junction of the Macaza and the Rouge Rivers, where for a month or more we camped in tents on a little level bench of land. This was a good spot, as a small farmer operated a hand-power ferry which made it possible to move a horse and wagon and allowed us to work both sides of the Rouge. We could drive a horse and buggy up the east side of the Rouge and ford it at a certain spot simply by driving the horse into it at a well-known shallow place, which saved a lot of miles and time.

Five miles above the camp on the west side and above the Twin Sisters Rapids, an interesting development was taking place.

An Italian *entrepreneur* named Vilani had leased a large tract of timber land from the Quebec government and, in anticipation of the railway extension, had brought out about seventy-five experienced, forest-trained men from the mountain slopes of northern Italy. These men from the north were fine, well-built loggers, many with fair hair and blue eyes, descendants of the Germanic hordes which had overrun Italy as far as Rome in the early centuries of the Christian era. They were quite unlike the southern Italians. On the river bank Vilani had built a large sawmill just above the rapids, and had been promised a railway. He must have been cutting pine and hauling it to the river for three years before we made an appearance. He had sawn millions of feet of pine, which was piled alongside the river road.

In the spring of 1903, while the promised railroad was actually being graded south and north of this point, we had arranged with Signor Vilani to move the lumber and logs he had piled on what was now the right of way bought by the CPR. This was done by what is known as "force work"; that is, actual cost of labour plus ten per cent for supervision. I was given the job of timekeeper. I was boarding at a hastily built and unfinished house nearby and sleeping in its attic at the time, but one day the Italian foreman invited me to have lunch with his men at a long table on the upper floor of the mill. The meal consisted largely of bread their own cook had baked plus cheese from Italy and light red wine from the same source. They cut their cheese with their long sheath knives. As an act of good manners they first spit on their knives and then wiped them clean on their overalls. The food was very good and I learned a few Italian words like "good morning" and "thank you very much". I liked these friendly men very much.

Forest fires were an ever-present threat until the woods got green, and after I left that day, the fires got into the huge piles of logs and lumber. Once started, nothing could stop them. Three years' work and a priceless amount of lumber went up in flames.

I heard about it that evening down at Labelle and early next morning I drove up on the river road opposite the mill. The heat was so great that I had to move downstream. It was a spectacle that is usually called an inferno.

Two alternatives for continuing the line past Vilani's mill presented themselves. The Rouge was the main river and a rough stream for most of its course. I heard a river driver say that there was a rapids every mile and that every rapids was named after some driver who had been drowned in them. The problem was that if we crossed the river and continued up the right bank, we would run right into the village of L'Annonciation, which was located, like so many river towns, right on the steep bank of the river on a shelf of land before it continued up the hill. The result was that the village had one street about a mile long. The railway would either have to run down the street, which the villagers vigorously opposed, or behind the row of stores and other buildings, which could only be done by a long, curved trestle. Another alternative was to run the line on the east or left side of the river where there was already a traffic bridge, an old covered one.

The villagers did not want to have to go down the hill and cross the bridge in order to reach the station. Mr. Garden argued with the council but in the end we had to run behind the stores. This was a horrible job, since the villagers for years had thrown all their garbage and the contents of their privies on the side of the riverbank. Through this mess we had to wade in order to survey the line, and this is where the trestle was eventually built.

By this time we had moved up to live in the hotel at L'Annonciation while we worked through thick pine forest towards Nominingue. The parish had built a fine church and a presbytery for the priest.

The village people had an interesting custom which we sometimes watched on Sunday morning. The post office was closed, of course, so the postmaster set up a table and chair on the street in front of the church and as soon as church was out, he would mount the table and start calling names from a handful of letters. As each name was called, somebody in the crowd would call *"Ici"* and come up for his mail. After the mail was delivered the town crier would make some announcements about lost cows and so on, and then the parisioners would visit with each other for a time before following their rough, tree-lined road home.

One day when we were working in heavy pine forest about half way to Nominingue we crossed a long muskeg. After reaching dry ground on the far side, we saw and smelled smoke on the trail we had just travelled. This meant a forest fire and a big one, judging by the amount of smoke and occasional flash of flame that we saw. Our retreat to the village was cut off. We ate our lunch while we figured what course to take.

Ben was in charge and ordered a left turn, walking west. After walking for about half an hour in the dark of the heavy bush, Ben turned left again, figuring that he had outflanked the fire. But I was sure that he was wrong, and a new member of our party named Hammersley, a Royal Military College cadet, agreed with me. We should have stuck together, even if we thought the leader was off the line, but we refused to go with Ben and took our own course. Half an hour later Hammersley found an old blaze on a big tree and, telling me to stand by it, he made a circle around the tree until he found another blaze. Then, by lining them both up, we saw faint signs of an old winter logging road.

It was almost dark now, but before long the bush thinned out a bit and we saw a light in a window. We hurried forward and found a young married couple, homesteaders, who received us kindly and asked us to have something to eat. I shall never forget that meal for it was by then about 9 p.m. and we had walked a long way and were ravenous. The bride set before us a plateful of pancakes with their own maple syrup and some fresh milk and bread, all of which we wolfed down with gusto. We then persuaded the young man to hitch up his horse and drive us to the village, for which we were glad to pay him.

We found out that the main party had not yet come in and when we reported our action to the chief we got a well-deserved bawling out. It was only human, however, that we should be highly pleased with ourselves for being right while Ben had been wrong. The group that followed him spent an uncomfortable night in the bush and Ben was sore when he came in.

The survey was finished by the end of August. The plans and profiles had been sent to head office in Montreal, and Mr. Garden asked me to stay on for a few days to help him close up the office. The students had to return to college and the axe men were paid off, but I was at a loose end. And speaking of pay, the rates were as follows:

Assistant engineer	per month	$150.00
Transit man		$100.00
Rod man		$ 40.00
Chain man		$ 30.00
Axe man		$ 30.00

In addition the company paid for our bed and board.

I read recently that the wages paid in the 1880s for similar work were the same, so that in twenty years there had been no increase whatever. Engineers used to say that the low salaries paid and the fact that they had to walk all over the country and were seldom at home made them nothing but educated tramps.

A few days after the members of the party left, the chief told me that the company had suddenly decided to commence construction in the spring and that they would be shipping the necessary materials to Labelle all winter. The ties would be supplied locally, but the company would send in all the rails, spikes, bolts, angle irons, bridge timbers from B.C. and all the stock necessary to build the stations, section houses and tool sheds. Then there were the needed fence posts and telegraph poles and the wire for both of them. We had to build a warehouse to store anything that might be damaged by the weather. The rails weighed sixty pounds to the yard and had been torn up from the main line, where they had been replaced by the new eighty-pound steel. As I knew shorthand, would I stay on and be his clerk and look after all this material? He would see Ovila Daoust, the section foreman, and get his release from the operating department so that Daoust could hire a gang of about thirty men, repair the three miles of track that had been abandoned and unload the material as it came at the end of track. My salary would be increased to forty dollars a month and I would live at Madame Renaud's, the best boarding house in the village.

Madame Renaud was an old widow who, rumour said, had suffered some severe shock earlier in life which distorted her face and made it twitch. But she kept a nice clean house and set a pretty good table, except that she had a penchant for serving fat pork twenty-one times a week. She also had a keen eye for making an extra dollar and to this end she divided her long, fairly commodious two-storey, French-Canadian house into as many bedrooms as possible. She did not even bother to put up partitions but simply divided one good room into two by means of a curtain. In this way she made four rooms upstairs into eight, and downstairs she managed to gain two more rooms by slicing some space off the living room. There was no heat in the house except for the kitchen range and one big wood burner in the dining room. All the hard work was done by a buxom *Canadienne "fille engagé"* called Marie Ange. I was secretly fascinated by Marie Ange, but too shy to make up to her.

I met Daoust the next day and took an instant liking to him. He had built railroads with Mr. Garden before and the CPR always made him available for extra-gang jobs. He spoke English but was illiterate, being able only to sign his name. When I met his wife a few days later I found her a capable, friendly woman, and six months later she spoke to the chief and offered her small front room as an office, which we gladly accepted. Then I moved in and she gave me a spare bedroom and excellent meals, a great improvement on Madame Renaud's. They had three small children who babbled away to me in French; it was, of course, beyond their comprehension that there was any other language.

Ovila was as tough as he looked with his prominent jaw. He could lick any man in the gang and they knew it, so there was never any doubt about who was boss. One day he said to me, "Let's go over to the village and see if I can pick up a couple of men." We went downhill and crossed the covered bridge, and entered one of the two hotels by the side entrance which led into a small room containing a few cheap little tables and chairs. We heard a noise in the hall; then a drunken lumberjack carrying a pitchfork charged into the room and aimed his barnyard bayonet right at

Ovila's middle. Nimble as a cat, Daoust picked up a light chair and smashed it over the man's head. The drunk collapsed in a corner. Finding no men in the bar, we left by the same door and saw our late opponent resting quietly where he had fallen.

On another occasion we were on the station platform waiting for the freight train to pull in. As the train stopped, two well-built but very grimy tramps crawled out from under a boxcar. They looked around and walked in to see the station agent, Mr. D'Amour. They soon came out, as the agent had told them to speak to Daoust if they wanted a job.

Daoust was sitting on an upturned keg of bolts, whittling on a piece of pine and smoking his pipe.

I sized them up, and decided that they were from Montreal and had been working in coal, judging by the fine black specks on their faces and their black clothing. They wore black felt hats with a few matches stuck in their hat bands. Times were hard in Montreal that winter, so they had come up to the end of steel to find work.

The bigger one said to Daoust, in English,

"Are you taking on any men?"

"Yes."

"What are you paying?"

"A dollar a day, and for good men, a dollar and ten cents."

Daoust intended no offence by this remark. What he meant was that for experts like spikers he would pay an extra ten cents a day.

The man made the mistake of supposing that the foreman was an ignorant rustic who didn't know the score, so he said sneeringly, "What do you know about good men?" Daoust never said a word. He quietly folded his jackknife and put it in his pocket. He knocked the ashes out of his pipe and put it in another pocket, and then he stood up and like a flash hit that mistaken man on the jaw so hard that he skidded across the platform and slid under a stationary boxcar. His pal helped him out. No more was said and we never saw them again. Ovila had just demonstrated one of his principles, and that was never to hire a man he couldn't lick.

It was hard to get workers, so one day the foreman said, "I'm going down to St. Jovite tomorrow to see if I can pick up some men. You run the gang."

On the following day I went up the line with the gang on two handcars. It was a crowd, but we managed by placing a couple of two-inch planks on the floor. Some men stood on them while others sat on the overhanging ends.

Our job that day was to load flatcars from piles of gravel alongside the track. The gang was a good one and I can still remember many of the names. In particular I remember the Corbeil brothers—tall, fair-haired, blue-eyed Normans—Renaud the carpenter, and little Joe Dufour, the clown of the gang who kept everyone laughing. He looked like a clown with his loose and too-long pants, which always looked as if they were about to fall down, and his little comical hat and a face that always wore a grin. Our waterboy was a cheerful lad of about fifteen years whose duty it was to carry a bucketful of cold water and a tin cup. Although every man in the gang was French, they invariably called "waterboy" in English when they were thirsty.

They were a happy gang too, and frequently sang as they worked. I spent six months with them and never had better or more versatile workers. During the next four years I worked with many European nationalities. The Swedes were the best rock drillers, drilling by hand and blasting, and the Italians can't be beaten for pick-and-shovel work, but I found that a French Canadian could turn his hand to anything. It was his pioneer training that made him so. Any man in our gang could load or unload heavy material and pile it skillfully, build a fence, make a culvert, fell a tree, drive a horse or a team, use an axe or a peavy expertly and do many other things besides.

However, we had one little black-eyed man who never stopped talking. I did not mind the talk, but every time he made a remark he leaned on his shovel, a thing he would never do if Daoust were present. At last I told him to stop talking and get to work. He looked at me insolently and said,

"This is not a school."

"No, you are right. This is a place to work, so get on with it."

"You are not the foreman."

"Mr. Daoust put me in charge for the day so you do what I tell you."

I was standing in the middle of the track when he walked up the bank with his shovel. The gang stopped to see what would happen. He lifted his shovel as though to strike me. I didn't budge but I didn't want to fight with him either. I had not been trained in the art of self-defence; I figured that if the shovel came down, I would try to catch it by the handle with my right hand and hit him with my left, but in the same instant a better idea came to me: I would try the Voice of Authority.

"Put that shovel down," I shouted. "You're fired. Now start walking."

He looked at me in astonished disbelief, too surprised to speak. The idea of a stripling like me . . .

He lowered the shovel and walked slowly to the fence where he had left his dinner pail in the long grass. Too embarrassed to face his fellow workers, he started slowly down the middle of the track. I had given him what railroaders call "a tie pass".

During my life in various vocations I have observed that a direct order given in a firm voice will be obeyed by men used to obedience when coaxing and argument are totally ineffective. Years later, I broke up a disturbance in the army that was rapidly developing into a riot by giving a direct order after persuasion had proved useless.

That night Daoust, back from St. Jovite, came in to see me in my bedroom.

"I hear you fired Martineau."

"Yes, I'm sorry about that because he is married and has two or three children and I guess he needs the job."

"You done right. He always talks too much. I'll let him sweat for a couple of days and then I'll take him on again."

It was our custom to go to work and return the three miles to the material yard on two handcars. It was always dark when we headed for home, so the foreman kept a sharp lookout and his foot on the brake.

There was no regular traffic on this stub line and no doubt the conductor and crew from the operating department thought that they had a clear track, but Daoust was too old a railroader to be caught without a light and he always carried a lighted lantern with him when homeward bound at night.

On one of these occasions, he suddenly yelled "Jump" and tramped on the brake, waving his lantern as he did so. We all jumped to the sides but the men were quick and whipped the handcars off the track by their handles just as the first boxcar loomed in front of us and then silently glided past.

A train of cars loaded with steel rails was being pushed ahead of the engine and a brakeman with a lantern should have been on the roof of the leading car. But the conductor had failed to live up to standard regulations and there might have been a serious accident, except for the foreman's quick action.

The engine driver stopped when he saw us and the conductor came running up to see what was the matter. Daoust then gave the assembled crews a dressing down in virulent French that drew apologies from the conductor and a promise to be more careful in the future.

One evening in the spring I walked up the track from the station at Labelle and came to a small mountain of solid rock. This I climbed, and from the top looked north up the River Rouge. The sun was setting and the sky was reflected in golden hues in the moving water. The dark woods on the other shore came right down to the water's edge. There was not a building in sight. A few logs floated lazily downstream. Occasionally a fish jumped for a fly or a kingfisher flitted about from log to log, looking for food. I thought that this noble little river, rising in some remote clear northern lake, had seen many generations of Indians carried on its bosom in their canoes to trade furs with the white man at Ville Marie. And long before the Europeans, they came to hunt and fish.

Generations of men have experienced the fascination of the North all around the world and I was one of them.

One cold moonlit winter night when I was still staying at Mme. Renaud's, I had gone to the station about 10 p.m. to get the official mail, which came by baggage car. The usual route home was to go down the station hill, along the riverside road and cross the bridge, but this night I decided to cross on the ice above the falls, the Chute aux Iroquois. This was a noisy waterfall, tumbling about thirty-five feet amongst great jagged rocks. A covered bridge had been built over it. I had often taken this short cut to save time, but now it was late March and the ice had begun to thaw. The path led over a small island in the middle of the stream, near the head of the waterfall. I crossed this and stepped over on to the river ice beyond when suddenly it gave way under me. I was in up to my neck.

At first I felt nothing and then the icy cold hit me. The swift current tugged at my feet. I scrambled back on to the island, soaked to the skin from head to toe. My wet clothing began to freeze and stiffen, and I knew I had to move rapidly.

There was no use in calling out, since the rumble of the falls made a voice inaudible at ten feet. At that time most people would be in bed, so I had to decide whether to stay there and freeze to death or try the ice farther up stream. I walked to the end of the little island and cautiously stepped on to the ice. It held to the far shore, where I climbed the bank and ran all the way home.

Fortunately Mme. Renaud had left the front door unlocked because she knew that I was working late. I made straight for the big stove in the dining room. The fire had been banked for the night, but I opened up the drafts and water soon ran off my clothing on to the floor.

Everybody was in bed, apparently, so I knocked on the door of the old lady's bedroom on the ground floor. She soon came out and exclaimed about her wet floor but she was a country-bred woman and quickly brought things under control. She called for Marie Ange who appeared in a dressing gown and began to mop up the floor, while Madame made me take off all my clothes except my long underwear, run upstairs, strip and rub down and jump into bed as fast as I could. Marie Ange took the wet clothes to be hung up behind the kitchen range; a few minutes later she reappeared at my bedside with a cup of hot tea. I soon became warm and dropped off to sleep.

Before I left home my father had given me only two

pieces of advice. One was not to go swimming alone. The other was to make friends with the cook. This advice was sound and except for the inadvertent dip described above, I followed it. If the cook is friendly he can make life a little more comfortable. For instance, he can let one dry his clothes behind the stove after a day in the rain, or he can provide a hot drink of tea and a biscuit at odd hours or some hot water for washing, or he can refuse these favours if he is not in a good humour. The cook rules the kitchen and let anyone beware of taking liberties; he need be afraid of no one because he always has two weapons handy: a pot of boiling water and a big butcher knife.

Lumbermen and railroaders have a saying that there are three cooks in every camp: one there, one going and one coming. It has always been hard to get satisfactory cooks for large camps. Probably there is something about standing over a huge kitchen range most of the day that gets on men's nerves and makes them irritable. The day starts early but for the cook it is earliest of all.

One very cold day in mid-winter when it was about twenty-five below zero, I received a message to meet the train, pick up a new cook for one of the line camps and take him up there, a drive of about nine miles. My only means of transportation was an old mare called Maud and a low *berlot*, or sleigh, built like a box with low, solid wooden runners and shod with steel bands, such as one sees in Kreighoff paintings. It had one double seat and a high dashboard to protect the driver from lumps of snow and ice flung backward from the mare's hoofs when she trotted, which was not often as she much preferred to walk.

The cook was ill equipped for such a journey in his city clothes, consisting of a lightweight overcoat, a felt hat and tight-fitting gloves. I told him that he had better tie his handkerchief around his ears or they would be frozen. I was comfortable in a heavy woollen toboggan cap pulled over my ears, a short woollen mackinac coat with a hood, heavy home-knit woollen mitts inside deerskin pullover mitts, my feet protected by four-buckle overshoes. We had a bearskin lap robe.

The roads were not ploughed in those days and the snow drifted unevenly into ridges across the road, so that our springless *berlot* climbed a succession of hogsbacks and slid down the other side, where we landed with a great bump before the mare toiled up the next slope.

Before long I saw that the end of the cook's nose was a dirty white, which contrasted with his natural flesh colour.

"Your nose is frozen," I told him. "You had better rub it."

"No, it isn't," he replied. "It never freezes."

"Well, it's your nose and if I were you I'd do something about it."

I was glad to be rid of him by the time we made camp, where I presume his nose was painfully thawed out.

The winter passed, and, with the disappearance of the snow, the land dried up and there was a great deal of activity. Several locomotives, vans (cabooses) and a string of flat cars were loaned to us by the operating department and came under the control of the construction department. Engine and train crews have to make out a trip ticket every day showing what they have been doing, mileage travelled and coal used. I now had to sign these tickets, so I got to know all the crews. I was a sort of unofficial, untrained master mechanic and trainmaster. The crews thought it was a great joke. I got to know all the train crews, who were invariably French although the engineers were often English. The same men were with us all summer and I used to like to listen to their shop talk. Most of them had run out of Montreal and had many stories to tell about wrecks or snowstorms that had held them blocked in cuts until rescued by a snowplough and an extra gang with snow shovels.

One day a group of train and engine men were standing on the platform at Labelle Station when a short freight train, known as an "extra", pulled in with a trainman standing on top of the leading boxcar according to regulations. On construction trains these formalities were disregarded.

"Look at the decoration," said Louis Denault, a brakeman noted for his heavy but perfectly formed black eyebrows. "They must be a main-line crew or else there's a boss on board."

Louis was right. As the train came to a stop, the division superintendent stepped down from the van, come to see how his boys were getting along in the construction department.

Then they sent me a little French car repairman named Laflamme. His duty was to make repairs on the spot instead of sending cars back to the shops in Montreal. Almost every day he came to me with a list of parts he wanted me to order. This was quite difficult because the names of the parts were in English; he could only talk French and he could barely write at all. So we had to puzzle them out, but we got along somehow and he did his work well. We gave him a little siding to himself where he wouldn't get run over. He further protected himself by showing a blue light, which means "man working underneath".

As early as 1750, the French-Canadian women were making a sash for men in a distinctly Canadian pattern. Its origin is obscure but its duplicate has not been found anywhere else. It is not Indian or Norwegian as many people have thought. But the French Basques and the Norwegians have made sashes that are somewhat similar.

The arrows used by the Indians were familiar to all French Canadians and are the dominant motif of the design,

The wool was imported from Scotland and woven into strands twisted extremely tight. These strands were as long as the sash including the fringe, or a total of fourteen to fifteen feet, and from eight to twelve inches in width.

The strands were braided, not woven, in a great variety of colours. Not having commercial dyes, the *Canadiennes* made the dyes from tree roots and plants, and possibly some coloured earths, and the results were always harmonious. The purpose of the sashes was to keep the body warm by gathering the blanket or buckskin coat tight about the kidneys.

By 1850 these *ceintures*, sometimes called "arrow belts" by the English, were very popular amongst the voyageurs of the fur trade and, in fact, the company partners. From there the fashion spread so that eventually no gentleman in Montreal or Quebec City considered himself properly dressed for winter wear unless he had one of these sashes tied around his overcoat at the waist. And of course many of the snowshoers of the various clubs wore them.

To make such a sash took a woman about three months. The strands were tacked to the wall about five feet from the floor, and then to the floor about seven or eight feet from the wall. The finished sash was often given as an engagement present to the girl's fiance.

Father had one when I was a boy and I longed for the time when I would be allowed to wear it. But he went to a fancy-dress party one night and as it grew warm in the hall, he took it off and hung it up in the cloak room; when he went for it, alas, it had been stolen. After that I dreamed of getting one for myself. The cabmen in Montreal used to wear them over their buffalo coats but tourists seemed to have bought them all up.

Now that I was in the centre of a French community at Labelle I thought my chances might be better. But this was new country being settled by young people; their possessions were fairly meagre and I never saw one anywhere. I told Daoust of my desire, but he had no information that he could give me.

Several months later, however, he came to me with a report that a clerk in Forget's store had one of these old sashes so I dropped in to see him. I told him of my interest and said that I understood he had one and asked if he would sell it. He was not interested in selling but offered to show it to me. He went to the back of the store and returned with a most beautiful sash in perfect condition. The arrowhead design ran down the centre in red and on both sides were the diamond-shaped sections in all colours and in subdued tones. The light blue was especially attractive and I was told that this dye was very hard to find.

The clerk told me that his grandmother had made it for his grandfather about seventy years before, and I believed him because that would be about 1830, when they were still being made by hand. Later, the fur companies had them manufactured by machine in England or Scotland and retailed them for four or five dollars. The cheap factory article drove the fine hand-made sashes off the market; the women stopped making them and did not pass the art on to their children, and so it became a lost art, although one or two people claim that they have mastered the technique anew.

The centre of the industry was in a French-Canadian village named L'Assomption not far from Montreal, where nearly every woman was engaged in this home handicraft, and if several women in one house were so engaged the men would complain that the room was so cluttered up with strands of wool that they could hardly get through. The belts picked up the name of the village because of the women's industry, and were often called L'Assomption belts or sashes.

I used to call at the store every month with my forty-dollar salary cheque, but the clerk was always firm and could not be moved. Then one day Daoust came to me and said, "That fellow Robillard in Forget's store is pretty hard up and I hear that he is thinking of selling his sash." For fear that I would be late I ran all the way to the store, and when he got through waiting on a customer I once more made my offer. To my delight, he agreed, and brought out the sash in return for my salary cheque.

They are to be seen in museums but hard to find for sale. Unfortunately they are not suitable for skiing so there is no demand except from collectors. Mine still hangs on the wall of my living room, admired by everyone.

I had one other opportunity to buy a sash but it was attended by failure. It had to do with the river drivers' custom of following the drive to its end, where they usually spent all their money on a big drunk and then, penniless, walked back home with their few possessions in a big handkerchief, for a hundred miles or more. One day while I was standing on the road at Vilani's sawmill by the Rouge, a solitary figure approached. He was dressed in the cheapest kind of clothing, work shirt and blue jeans, but as he got closer I saw that he was wearing the most beautiful sash I had ever seen. It had the appearance of silver due to the clever mixture of predominant light grey with soft tones of light blue and green. I stopped and admired his sash, for I guessed correctly that he was penniless and might sell. I started by offering him five dollars, but he said that the sash was not for sale. I kept raising my bid until I got up to fifty dollars. It could hardly be called bargaining, as he had made clear his decision at the beginning that he was not interested.

Finally he said, "Look, *m'sieu*, my grandmother made this *ceinture* and it is not for sale. I know that I am broke but you can keep your fifty dollars. *Au revoir*."

I regretted his decision, but I admired his spirit.

3 RIVER DRIVERS

When the snow melts in April it naturally runs into the many little streams and bigger rivers of the whole country from the international boundary to the sub-arctic, and high water is what the loggers want. All winter long they have been stacking their logs on the lake ice and on the riverbanks and even on sizable creeks, ready for the great shove when the ice goes out.

The logs go floating and rumbling and falling down rapids and over waterfalls in countless thousands. Every log has been branded with a marking hammer by a "culler" (inspectors who cull the logs into various grades). The brand marks are on the ends so that when the logs reach a sorting boom they can be separated according to ownership. Then they are collected in booms and towed to the mill where they will be sawn. In the River Rouge country, their destination would likely be Hawkesbury on the mighty Ottawa where there were large mills.

The Rouge, by the way, gets its name from its colour. It is perfectly clear and good tasting but red as tea. Many northern streams are so coloured for a great variety of reasons, vegetable and mineral, in the territory they drain, that have nothing to do with pollution by industry or sewage. I once disgraced myself on survey by throwing out a pail of tea, thinking it was river water.

When the logging camps close in the spring and the horses are sent home with their farmer-owners or to a big company farm where feed is raised and pasture provided, the foreman of the drive retains the men he wants, and who want to stay to ride the logs one hundred miles or more to their sawmill destination.

This was dangerous and exciting work. Only the most expert and fearless men· were chosen, and they had their pay increased ten dollars a month above the winter wage. Every boy on the river wanted to be a driver when he grew up. Barefooted, they played "river driver" on big logs floating near the riverbank, learning balance and timing for their jumps.

As long as the water was high, the logs rode easily downstream, but some were bound to get caught in eddies or stranded on rocks so the drivers had to keep them moving. To do this they rode the logs through smooth water, the long sharp caulks or spikes on their low oil-tanned boots enabling them to keep their balance. They were frequently in water over their knees so that there was no point in wearing high boots in an attempt to keep dry; the low boots, if filled with water, could quickly be emptied, like slippers. Their dress was usually colourful, with gay hats, sometimes red or black with a feather stuck in them, or perhaps a knitted wool toque; bright-coloured shirts; pants chopped off at the knee (long pants would get soaking wet and would impede movement); and then long, heavy wool stockings tied with brightly coloured, tasseled garters. A few wore the machine-made sash, cheap but gay.

These French Canadians were probably the best white-water men in the world.

Their day started about 5 a.m. with a big hot breakfast consisting largely of beans mixed with pork, bread and tea. The beans were cooked in the best possible manner to retain their flavour. The cookee would first dig a hole about two feet deep in the sand. In this a fire would be laid and lighted. When the hole got really hot, the cook would lower a shallow but very wide iron pot full of beans mixed with chunks of pork and flavoured with molasses. The pot was covered with a heavy iron top, which had a flange to keep the sand out. As soon as the pot was lowered into the red-hot embers it was covered with sand. The beans cooked all night and came out in the morning yellow as gold.

Madame Daoust used a variation of this plan at home. She took her pot of beans to the baker next door and he would keep it in his hot oven all night, a service for which he made no charge. In the morning Madame would nip into the bake shop, recover her beans, and we would all enjoy them for breakfast.

Work started on the logs near their camp. The drivers often had to wade right into ice-cold water to get at their task and move the logs that had become stationary during the night. To get them moving, they used a stout pole with a hook and a spike on the end called a peavy, with which they could roll the logs or push them on their way.

As soon as the cook could clean up, he and his assistant, or cookee, would load a long riverboat pointed at each end and called a "pointer", not unlike the York boats used by the Hudson's Bay Company on the rivers in the far northwest. These useful boats were flat bottomed and could poke their noses in anywhere due to their gracefully pointed bows, and sterns sloped back to the flat bottom. The point could float over logs or be beached without upsetting. The cook and cookee would row or pole this craft downstream until they passed the drivers, or came to a spot where they should be approaching around 9 a.m. There they would land and prepare some hot tea and a snack for the wet and hungry men, and move on again.

The work went on until dark, and the crew usually ate five times a day as they worked long hours and burned up a lot of calories.

I mention the work of the river drivers, which was outside my scope of activity, because we worked alongside them on the riverbank and near the many rapids during the day. In the evening we saw the lumberjacks at work at the log jams in the falls.

It was thrilling to see these nimble-footed men running along the slippery logs and untangling them if they got jammed. The Chute aux Iroquois at Labelle was a serious obstacle with its huge rocks, and jams frequently formed there. Drivers would run out quickly, as soon as they saw a jam beginning to form, and try to pry the logs apart before the jam got too large. When the jam began to move and rushing water poured through, they had only seconds to run from moving log to log in order to reach shore safely. Sometimes they didn't make it, and another driver's name would adorn a rough wooden cross by the riverside.

If the jam was too large to move by hand, the foreman was usually the man who went out to as near the centre as he could get with a few sticks of dynamite and a long fuse. He would wedge the explosive between two logs and carry the fuse back towards shore where he would light it with a match. In a few minutes the pile of logs would fly into the air and the whole mass that had been blocking the river would heave and tumble downstream.

Logs are usually trucked or railed to market now and only four-foot pulpwood is floated down the rivers. The last drive of logs down the Gatineau River, for instance, took place in 1925, although they still drive some down the Lievre, twenty miles down the Ottawa River.

I was interested to learn that, in the old days, at the time of Maisonneuve's rule in Montreal and those who succeeded him during the seventeenth century, bands of Iroquois warriors from what is now part of New York State would enter Canada by Lake Champlain and the Richelieu River and attack the French at the small fort and settlement at Montreal; they would then proceed farther up the Ottawa River to intercept bands of friendly Algonquians and Hurons coming downstream from faraway Lake Huron with furs to trade with the French. The Iroquois were eastern North America's fiercest warriors and unfortunately had been feuding with the French since the latter first settled around the island of Montreal, while the Algonquins had always been friendly. The Iroquois operated far north of their home territory, penetrating as far as the region where Ottawa stands today. A number of turbulent rivers flow into the Ottawa from the north side and one of these was the Rouge. The hostile Iroquois paddled their war canoes up the Rouge for eighty-five miles, killing and robbing the peaceful Indian inhabitants and taking prisoners. They reached at least as far as the waterfall at present day La-belle, and for many years this spot was called by the French *Chute aux Iroquois*. In time the French pioneers began to call the place *Lachute*, but as Quebec became more settled the name became confused with another and older Lachute near Montreal, so the government changed the name to La-belle after the famous Roman Catholic missionary of that name.

When a gang of rivermen hit a town like Labelle after being confined to a camp in the woods for five months, and with their winter's pay unspent, they cast aside all re-straint and went on a wild spree. They drank raw *whiskey blanc*; soon arguments led to fights, and the battles that followed raged all over the hotel and out on to the street. They used no weapons such as knives or revolvers like the wild westerners in the States, but made deadly use of their spiked boots as well as their fists. The Marquis of Queens-berry rules were unknown. If a man was floored by a blow, they considered that that was the best time to attack him with their spiked feet. They jumped on his body and used spikes to rake his face so that many of these men bore the scars of such combat to their graves. In some hotels the managers forbade the wearing of spiked boots, not from any humanitarian motives but to prevent their floors from being ripped up. Some were kind enough to provide cheap carpet slippers at the door.

I saw a number of these fights and narrowly escaped becoming involved in them when we were guests at the hotel in L'Annonciation. One day I saw a man plunk down his winter's pay-cheque and say to the bartender "Tell me when to stop." Then he started in to break the big mirror behind the bar by throwing heavy glasses at it. Another man satis-fied his urge for destruction by taking the piano stool by the legs and smashing all the keys off the piano.

The worst fights occurred when gangs from rival lumber companies struck town at the same time, having come from converging streams. The McLarens and the Riordans were two of these companies. They thought nothing of walking five miles after work, spending a riotous evening and then walking back to camp and arising at 5 a.m. the next morning. In those days there were no police in the small settlements and few in Hull or Ottawa, and they were wise enough to keep clear of these riots.

I could not understand why a man would work hard all winter and spring for this doubtful satisfaction of a few minutes.

At last, Labelle's Hotel du Nord burned down one night. The whole gang, friends and foes, disregarding everything else, saved the long bar and as much liquor as possible and carried it all across the covered bridge to an empty barn, where business was resumed with lightning-like rapidity.

I was staying at the hotel in L'Annonciation that spring; one evening, as I went down the main stairs which ended near the front door, a young river driver saw me and stood squarely in my path.

He was a little drunk but just enough to make him talkative. What was more important was his height and girth, as he stood at least six feet and had powerful-looking arms and shoulders. And he wore those terrible spikes on his boots! He could have eaten me alive. I certainly did not want to tangle with him. Diplomacy would be best, I thought.

I said to him civilly, in French,

"Let me pass please, I want to go out."

He did not move but began to make fun of my clothing. My corduroy breeks especially amused him.

I said nothing but just stared him in the eye.

Eventually he ran out of words to express his contempt for my attire and I repeated my request that he let me pass.

Suddenly his mood changed. He became the court jester.

Stepping aside, he placed his left hand on his heart, bowed low and, sweeping his right hand towards the door he said,

"Passez m'sieu."

I tried to play up by making a regal exit, but the effect was rather spoiled because of my inner feeling that I would receive a kick in the pants as I passed this bully boy of the Rouge. I glanced back, but he just stood there laughing.

"Of all the outrages perpetrated on the small boy, formal dress was the worst . . .

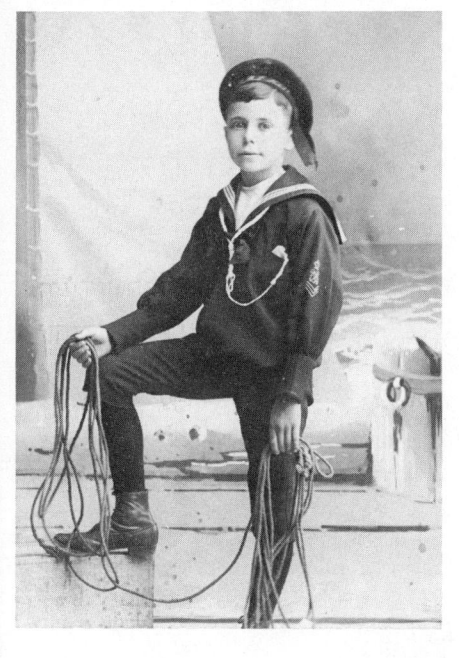

The sailor suits weren't too bad . . .

but the Little Lord Fauntleroy suit was '2 mutch'."

Standing – Mr. Duncan S. Macintyre, St. George Snowshoe Club (about 1885).

umberjacks at work on a log drive in northern Quebec, 1927.

he mouth of the Bear River on the upper Ottawa.

A hand car.

A pile driver during the construction of false work for a bridge.

trestle similar to the one at l'Annonciation.
typical rock cut, this one in the Crow's Nest Pass, 1898.

CPR 239 — the first coal burner.

Laying track for the CPR on the prairies.

racklaying with a derrick west of Edmonton, 1912.

rading on the CPR; steam shovel at right.

The Fort William yards, 1902.

Three locomotives hauling a heavy train up the grade near Credit Forks, not far from Bolton.

4 FOREST FIRES

Forest fires were widespread that spring of 1903. In those days there was no forest protection service against these conflagrations; no fire towers with telephones, no motor boats or cars and no airplanes. The fires either burned themselves out or were quenched by rain. Fires seemed to keep rain away and burned for weeks. It was a country of evergreens, or coniferous trees, and they ignite quickly. The dry slash from lumber cuttings and natural pruning of the branches made it easy for fire to travel quickly along the ground. If a fire ran up the tree and then jumped to the surrounding tree tops it was called a crown fire and was impossible to extinguish by old-time methods. The heat of the great fires made its own wind and spread it faster.

The village of Labelle was nearly destroyed that year.

Fires were burning all around us so that we never saw the sun for six weeks. The bald rocky hill opposite the station, which had been burned over many times until one would think there was nothing left to burn, was blazing like live coal. Even the soil burned.

On the west or opposite side of the river, where most of the village was located, the fire was getting closer. The *curé* had ordered the church bell to be tolled continuously in alarm because the rather imposing church building was in peril.

Ovila had gone down the line to Conception, the next station, to help Jerry Carriere, the section foreman, because the station and nearby bridge were in danger. A car on the siding, loaded with valuable American anthracite coal amounting to about thirty tons, burned to the tracks and after that glowed with red-hot coals for days.

I thought that the village was doomed. I put all my office papers in the tin breadbox that I used as a safe, took it down to the river's edge and put it in the shallow water, leaving only the lid exposed but held down with a small rock.

Madame Daoust and the three children were at home and she was naturally perturbed about the safety of the house, so I suggested that we at least keep the roof wet. We worked out a pretty useful plan. They had a good well in the yard, close to the kitchen door, and lifted water on a windlass and rope tied to a wooden bucket. I told her to get all the blankets she could find and to get the children — Hector, the eldest, at any rate — to help. I found a ladder and laid it against the house on the side exposed to the wind, and between us we hauled up water by the pail and soaked the blankets. I carried the wet blankets up the ladder and spread them on the roof. We had enough to cover it. Some sparks were blowing our way by now but our precautions probably saved the house.

About that time some official from the church came running up in a panic to see me. He wanted to know if I couldn't get some men from the railroad to help them fight the fire by the only method left: shovelling sand on it. My chief had taken the old grey mare that morning and gone up the line, so I had to make the decision. I decided that the CPR would not like having the village destroyed, since it had a population of about five hundred people and that meant a sizable amount of revenue in terms of freight.

I knew that we had a gang of about fifty men working in a gravel pit about three miles up the line and that they had a locomotive and a string of flat cars, so I climbed on my bicycle and rode out there on the dusty sand road. I had no authority and did not know who would pay the contractor for his men's time. But I must have been pretty convincing, for the foreman ordered his men to jump on the flatcars with their shovels and I told the freight conductor to run to Labelle as fast as the track would permit. I threw my bicycle on one of the flatcars and joined them. Charlie Alexander, the eagle eye on the 452, must have made a record run for the men were soon spilling off the flats and running downhill with their shovels and then up the hill on the other side of the river. They worked hard all afternoon and, while they didn't put the fire out, they held it in check until the village men came home from work.

Of course the contractor submitted an account for the labour he had supplied. The account came to me in the mail and I took it to the clerk of the council, or to the mayor, I forget which. The council, now that the danger was over, refused to pay it. How soon people forget their obligations once they are safe! Had I been more experienced I would have demanded a guarantee first, on the day of the fire when I held all the cards, but I was only eighteen and knew nothing of law. I foolishly thought that they would be glad to pay out of gratitude. It is by incidents such as this that a man gains experience.

I then sent the account to head office and in a few days got a summons to attend at the legal department of the CPR, so I packed a bag and reported to the lawyer in Montreal who had written me the letter. He was a pleasant and understanding fellow and asked me to tell him the story in my own words. When I had finished he smiled and said, "You may go back to Labelle now. I don't think that you will hear any more about this." We shook hands and I left, enormously relieved that I had not been fired for incurring expense without authority. Obviously they were not going to law with a group of good customers.

I did think, though, that the village might at least have passed me a vote of thanks.

Shortly after the near destruction of Labelle by fire, I had to drive up the west-side river road to L'Annonciation. The sky was overcast and the space between sky and ground was enveloped in heavy smoke, but I saw no flame until I reached a point about six miles from my destination. Here I could see fire stealing closer on each side of the road. I looked back and saw patches of flame here and there through the smoke, so that the only thing to do was to go ahead as fast as the old mare could trot.

The country I was moving through was being settled by people eager for land but, unlike the prairies, their land was to a large extent covered by virgin forest that included immense stands of white pine. The white pine enjoyed an immediate market and was eagerly sought after because of its height and girth and its suitability for construction purposes, for interior finishing and trim, sash and doors and many other uses. Much of it was exported to the United States and Europe.

As in the earliest times in North America, the homesteader had to clear his land before he could plant his crops. First he would fell the trees on about ten acres. Even this small area presented a herculean task because, after the trees were cut down by hand with an axe and the marketable logs had been hauled to the nearest sawmill or piling yard, the branches had to be burned. These brush fires often got out of control and spread to the surrounding forest. In fact, many settlers were not above setting fire to the forest in order to hasten their land clearing. Sometimes these fires ranged for miles and caused incalculable damage to life and property.

The hardest of all tasks was the rooting out of the stumps. Some ingenious stump pullers were invented and manufactured locally, but for the most part men had to dig around the roots and cut them one by one, often hindered by large stones embedded in them. At last, after perhaps a full day spent on one stubborn stump, a team of horses or oxen would pull it out and drag it away to the edge of the clearing where it formed part of a rough fence.

I often wondered why these settlers did not go out west where they would have no clearing problem, and I discussed this matter with several farmers.

Their reasoning was that they preferred to stay with their own people, and that they liked the opportunity of winter work for cash wages provided by the lumber companies, who were also willing to hire their horses. The forest provided them with the timber for their log buildings, cleverly notched at the corners with an axe, and with all their fuel, which the prairies could not do. The forest also supplied a family with meat in the form of deer and bear and small game. Game laws meant nothing to these farmers; they considered that such laws were made for city sportsmen only. They had heard that the prairie was a dry country, but here there was cold and pure water in plentiful supply, and nearby streams and lakes gave them all the fish they wanted. With all the advantages, they considered themselves better off than the wheat farmers of the western provinces.

But I saw the price some of them paid for the advantage of living in the forest, as I drove that day to L'Annonciation. I came to a homestead with about twenty-five acres cleared. The pioneer had built a neat log house near the road, according to custom, and had long piles of split cordwood neatly stacked in readiness for the next winter. His farm was divided from the next one by a split-cedar rail fence. This fence was on fire for at least one hundred feet, and the fire had spread to some of his wood piles, which were now blazing.

The poor man and his wife and little children, too exhausted to do more, had knelt down with their hands clasped and their heads bowed in prayer.

My inclination was to stop and help them, but I did not dare because if I lost time here I might not get through to the village myself. In any case, such help as I could give would be of little value, now that the rail fences on both sides of the public road were burning.

Similar scenes met my view before I escaped from the fire zone. Such fires were one of the ever-present risks of homesteading in the north woods.

5 THE MACDONALD CLAN

I learned early in the fall that the contract for grading the railway had been awarded to D. R. Macdonald and Co., a firm from Glengarry, Ontario. Mr. Macdonald and some of his staff came in early to look over the ground and were soon followed by others who began to organize the project, building camps at strategic locations and so on. The senior members stayed at Madame Renaud's also and amongst them was Jim McDonnel. Like most of the Macdonalds, McDonalds or McDonnells (they are all from the same clan)

71

Jim was a tall, broad-shouldered Highlander from Nova Scotia, and I think a cousin of D.R.'s. He also brought along his pleasant-looking bride of a few weeks on what I suppose was a honeymoon. He was to be walking boss on the whole job and was called "Jim the Walker". There were so many Macdonalds with the same Christian names that they had to be recognized by their initials or nicknames. For instance, D. R. was the son of D. D., but had three brothers who sometimes worked with him. One of these was Hughie D. D. His own son was called Hughie D. R. Angus McDonnel was the bookkeeper and was called Red Angus. The foreman in charge of the explosives was Daniel, known as "Dynamite Dan". Then there were Long Ranalds and Black Ranalds and many others.

I stayed at a camp of theirs once that winter while I did a time-keeping job on some work nearby and shared a hut for the night with Dynamite Dan. As I was getting into bed, I was surprised to see Dan putting a dozen sticks of dynamite in the oven of the box stove to keep them from freezing. I said, "Aren't you afraid you'll blow us into the Twin Sisters Rapids in the middle of the night?" He said, "No, there is no danger. You can burn them up without an explosion. They have to be hit with something." He left the door of the oven open, so that he could see how they were getting along during the night, I suppose.

These Macdonalds were an interesting group. There seemed to be no end to them, so I asked Angus how many Macdonalds they had brought with them. He said, "Wait a minute and I'll look up the pay book." So he got the book and counted. "One hundred and fifty-seven," he announced.

It was like a gathering of the clan in the Highlands of Scotland where all their ancestors had been born. They still retained some traces of their Scottish ancestry in their speech and manners; for instance, when eating oatmeal porridge, long Jim the Walker had a glass of milk placed beside his plate and then, instead of pouring milk over his porridge, dipped each spoonful in the milk after the Highland custom.

As the clan Macintyre is of ancient origin and is closely connected with the clan Macdonald, I was accepted as one of the set.

When the loyalist Scots came to Canada from the Mohawk Valley of the state of New York after the Revolutionary War of 1776, it was determined by the Canadian authorities that the Macdonalds and other clansmen and their families would be settled on the banks of the St. Lawrence River, in the new county of Glengarry adjoining the province of Quebec and named after their homeland parish. Each soldier was given one hundred acres, and there were gifts of a cow, food, seed and implements, to each family.

The soil of Glengarry is fertile but the land was covered then with giant trees, especially the pine which was in great demand in England. Although most of the clansmen were farmers originally, lumbering was more important in Glengarry than farming at first, and the splendid heavy Clydesdale horses they had brought with them proved to be useful in the winter in the logging operations. Many of the clansmen learned to be expert loggers and river drivers who took their squared timber rafts to Quebec for trans-shipment to England. They became prosperous and in a very few years, through energy and perseverance, had built roads and churches and schools and set up municipalities.

As Highland regiments were disbanded, many of their members settled in Glengarry; thousands of others in conducted parties came to Canada and, of these, many proceeded to the same county. Large numbers of Macdonalds and other Scots settled in Nova Scotia, many of them in Cape Breton.

In spite of their hardships over many years in Scotland, the fact that they were free men standing on their own land and doing well restored the Highlanders to their former health and strength and stature. All over Canada there was a saying, "As big as a man from Glengarry."

They were remarkably stalwart men, known all over Canada for their ability as well as for their size and strength. Many men notable in public life and in the two world wars have come from Glengarry. For instance, Donald Robert Macdonald was twice elected to his provincial legislature, both before and after I met him. He was a big burly man with a heavy mustache who only visited the job occasionally. And the men who came to build the railway at Labelle were worthy examples of their race.

The grading of the right-of-way went on all summer. The soil was sandy and easy to move with a team of horses and a wheeled or slush scraper. There was not much rock; in fact, the only sizable rock cut I remember was just south of the bridge that was thrown over the Rouge at its junction with the Macaza.

When a swamp or muskeg had to be traversed, long stakes were driven in a line, and then the fill, consisting of sand, gravel and rock, had to be dumped on the line, about sixteen feet wide, where it sank and pushed the soft, wet subsoil to each side. This continued until the fill found solid bottom and then gradually rose to the required grade. This left a mound of wet earth on either side pushed out by the pressure of the new fill. The surplus earth had to be removed and the space ditched to collect water, which was then carried away to both sides in smaller ditches dug at right angles to the grade. It was hard, dirty work.

Water is always a threat to railroad or highway builders and must be turned aside by culverts and ditches. Even the ballast under the tracks must be sloped outwards to direct rainfall away from the rails.

When a river had to be crossed, a careful study was

made to ascertain what type of structure or structures would be most economical and satisfactory, how many were required and what techniques would be used in assembling and erecting them. The most efficient bridge for the average stream in the period from 1900 to 1920 was the Howe truss, because it could be largely constructed of enormous timber beams, which were relatively cheap in those days, and because it used a minimum of steel. To span a shallow river, temporary piling was driven in rows and capped with square timbers. Across these pile bents, heavy timbers called stringers were cantilevered from shore to shore. These were placed on top of the pile bents to support a working floor; then excavations were made for the piers and the concrete poured into them.

It was then time to bring in the large timber beams and other materials and fittings to form the Howe truss bridge. The structure was built almost in place and, by the time it was complete, the pier concrete was usually strong enough to carry the bridge load. The structure was then slowly lowered, usually only a few inches, to its permanent place on the concrete.

One end of each span was rigid, but the other was left free so that expansion and contraction could take place normally, after each span was in its place. Eventually the falsework was removed and the bridge was ready for use. While work on the span could, and often did go on all winter, the falsework had to be removed before the spring flood, when high water and floating ice came downstream.

The contract for the erection of the bridge was awarded to John Brown, who had had long experience with this type of structure. When the timbers arrived from British Columbia, he laid out a framing yard.

Working from detailed plans whereon every piece was numbered, his workmen, or bridge carpenters, skilled in the use of adze and axe, sawed each piece to the proper length and notched it in the right places and at the right angles so that two related pieces would fit together perfectly. They were held firmly in place by large and long bolts.

A bridge is the first part of a new railway to be finished ready for the rails. Ordinary track ties are not needed; the rails are spiked directly to the bridge ties, and no gravel ballast is required.

A young man named Sutherland had the contract for the excavation of the rock hill nearby.

Dynamite had come into use but there was still a good deal of black powder employed. All drilling was done by hand, one man holding a steel drill and two strikers hammering at it all day long with alternate strokes. The holder would twist the drill a little with each blow. When they had gone deep enough they would stop, and a certain amount of black powder would be poured in.

One day when Sutherland himself was leaning over the hole superintending this operation, the powder exploded, blowing him up in the air so that he was dead when he landed. The two strikers and the holder were seriously injured. It was supposed that a spark from a previous blast had not been extinguished when the powder was poured in.

Sutherland was a fine-looking young man and had been highly regarded. That night, as I drove up to pay my respects, it was raining and blowing and it seemed to me that even Nature was weeping. He was laid out on his rough bunk, awaiting the arrival of the undertaker.

This was an isolated case, but it must be remembered that hundreds of men gave up their lives all across Canada in order that you and I might ride in ease and safety. Years later, during the First World War, shell bursts and resulting casualties brought back to me memories of the explosions in the rock cuts of the great Laurentian Shield.

By midsummer D'Aoust was laying track with CPR crews of experienced men. The practice was to make up a train of about ten flatcars loaded with ties, rails, bolts, spikes and angle irons. The train was loaded at the material yard and pushed ahead by the locomotive. At the forward end there was a derrick. Along each side of the train, rollers were attached; the derrick would lift the rail and a man would guide it to the rollers with a rail hook. The rail was then lowered by the derrick and started on its way by the rollers. On the other side, ties would be lifted by hand onto the rollers, as they came to the end, two men would grab them, lay them across the grade about two feet apart and line them up by stakes, for some distance ahead of the rails. Then six men would catch the first rail and carry it forward with rail thongs, lay it on the ties and then catch and lay a second rail. These rails would be bolted to the last one laid through the angle irons and so held together. The foreman would then have the gang line up the rails with lining bars and keep them equidistant by means of a metal gauge. When the rails were straight, the spikers would pound the spikes into the flange of the rail. They used a ten-pound spiking hammer; it took a good man like Ovila Corbeil to swing one of those ten hours a day, so he certainly earned his extra ten cents.

Spikes and bolts came forward by the same assembly line and were distributed by men or boys along the ties, so that no time was lost. It was considered a good day's work to lay a mile a day. A few years later, when rails for the Grand Trunk Pacific were being laid on the prairie on a tangent (straight line), they sometimes got two miles a day laid. After the main line was laid, another gang followed up and cut the rails at the required places for sidings, and switches were put in. The engineers prepared for this by providing a number of wide places in the grade.

As soon as we could get work trains running, we had overcome the transportation problem of getting building materials and such things as fencing and telegraph poles and wire up to the front. Tracklaying was followed quickly by ballasting. Gravel would be hauled from the pit, trains would be stopped while a huge metal unloader would be dragged the length of the train by a cable with steampower supplied by the locomotive. It acted like a snowplough and pushed the gravel over the edges to the ground. The train then went back to the pit for another load while a large gang of about one hundred men would fall on the gravel with their shovels, throw it onto the track and then tuck it under the ties and tamp it tight to keep the ties in place and the rails from moving. The foreman maintained levels with a long levelling board.

One Sunday when the line was clear we organized the distribution of telegraph poles. We had loaded the cars on Saturday. A labour gang of about thirty Italians was warned to be on hand the following morning. Since the train and engine crews spent the summer at Labelle, many of them had brought their wives up to be near them; no other work was going on just then so some of the trainmen brought their wives along in the van and made a little holiday of it to relieve the tedium. The train pulled out to the beginning of track and poles were thrown off at the right intervals until the cars were all empty. The train stopped then and an hour's halt was ordered. It was a beautiful summer day and all hands and the ladies rested on the grass and ate their lunches.

Going back, the engine had to run tender first and push the flatcars ahead. The track had not yet been ballasted with gravel, so was uneven and the locomotive had to run slowly. The Italians gathered on the foremost flatcar, their feet hanging over the sides. There is always one clown in a party and ours was no exception; one fellow who was a bit of an acrobat commenced doing handsprings and back flips to the applause of his friends. The conductor sent a trainman ahead to tell him to stop as it was dangerous, but in a few minutes he was performing again. Then it happened. The end car lurched at a depression in the rough track and the car became uncoupled. When this happens to a train the air brakes go on immediately in emergency. The train stopped with a violent jolt and then ran forward a few feet. The acrobat was operating too near the end and the jolt threw him overboard and ahead — he fell in the path of the train and, when it recoiled, as though on a spring, it ran over the unfortunate man and killed him. Few of the Italians spoke any English so it was impossible to explain to them the mechanics of what had happened; they thought that the engineer had stopped the train on purpose as a lesson to the Italians or to make the ladies laugh.

They lifted their comrade on board and returned to the station, but they were in a murderous mood.

That night they all came storming up to my little office and I tried to explain to them in my inadequate French that we were all very sorry and that an official from Montreal would be up in the morning. The official came; I do not know what was done but I do know that our engineer carried a heavy revolver in the bib of his overalls for some weeks after.

That winter, after the long curved trestle following the bend of the River Rouge was built at L'Annonciation, we laid track to Lac Nominingue and halted there while a bridge was being built across a narrows between two parts of the same lake. The bridge builders had to drive sheet piling to keep the water out and then fill the space with concrete. They had to use a pile driver and a diver for this work to make abutments for the ends of the bridge.

One day a work train was passing over the long trestle at L'Annonciation when, for some reason now forgotten, the locomotive became uncoupled from its train and fell off the trestle on to the river ice near the shore. Miraculously, the engineer and the fireman got out of the cab and walked unhurt over the ice to safety.

The problem then was how to get the locomotive back on the trestle, which was not much damaged and soon repaired.

They brought the pile driver down from Nominingue and used it as a derrick. Now a pile driver is a high, ungainly thing and the top of a narrow curved trestle is not an ideal platform from which to operate it; to our dismay, the strain pulled the machine off the trestle so that it fell with a crash to the ice and lay beside the engine. The operator had leapt free before the fall.

Now we were in more trouble than ever. The civil engineer in charge wired Montreal and they sent up a completely equipped wrecking train and crew who, after a long struggle, got both locomotive and pile driver raised.

An accident of this kind could ruin a small contractor, but a large corporation like the CPR took it in stride.

During the winter the company sent out another survey party which passed us and went on to Nominingue to run a reconnaissance line through the bush to Mont Laurier, about thirty-five miles north and west. When they came out in the spring, one of the party told me that there were people in there who had never seen a train.

I saw the first train arrive at L'Annonciation. A great crowd was on hand to see this marvellous machine, which puffed and snorted and rang a bell and blew a whistle and pulled a string of luxurious-looking coaches at great speed along the smooth track. It was said that these coaches were actually heated in winter. No longer would the settlers have to endure the long cold drives by road to visit friends and relatives in other villages.

As soon as the train stopped, those who had tickets pressed forward, fearing that the train might depart before they had a chance to embark and claim their seats. The train crew had to hold them back and reassure them.

This was what all our trouble and toil and loss of life had been about; that people could ride more comfortably and at greater speed.

A bridge and building gang arrived, and erected and painted the stations and section houses and other buildings by midwinter. I was living in a boxcar at L'Annonciation that winter and had my office in the same car. I boarded with a married couple nearby who also took care of about six working men. When Lent came Madame told me that, being good Roman Catholics, no meat would be served, but I told her that I was a Protestant and did not feel bound to observe this rule of their church. While I did not mind eating fish two or three times a week, I said, I must have some meat; so she agreed.

Theirs was a small house where the front door opened directly into the combined living, dining room and kitchen. One day at lunch time as we all sat at table, the local priest burst in without knocking and walked directly up to our table. He looked at everyone's plate. They all contained fish except mine. He looked at me with anger and asked if I was one of the faithful. I said, "No, I am a Protestant and I don't have to eat fish every day." I was as annoyed as he was and I am afraid that I was barely polite. He stalked out and slammed the door.

I respect the beliefs of the Catholic Church but I did not like being spied upon. Madame was, of course, embarrassed by the whole incident.

There can be no doubt that the church exercised a

powerful grip on the lives of its parishioners, in a way no Protestant would tolerate. The priests were devoted men for the most part and spent their celibate lives in service to their flock, according to what they had been taught and believed. Many lived out their existence in remote settlements ministering to a people of much more primitive culture than themselves. In these places it was a life of sacrifice, for which they hoped that the reward would be Heaven, but in larger towns and cities they not only lived more comfortably, but sometimes in semi-luxury with good food and obedient servants.

The local blacksmith, an intelligent fellow, to whom I occasionally took a bundle of tie picks to be sharpened for the extra gang, told me that he wanted to send his eldest son to an English school in Montreal so that he could learn English and be fitted for a better job when he grew up. The priest had heard of this ambition and went down to the smithy where he told the smith that he forbade it, and further, that if he persisted he might have to face excommunication. So the boy did not get his chance, and the smith was naturally resentful or he would not have poured out this story to me, a Protestant.

Large families were the rule. Many women had a baby every year. The station agent's wife had twelve at the time I was there. Jerry Carriere, the section foreman, told me that he was one of twenty-six children and that his mother had died at the age of thirty-nine. She must have had several sets of twins and been married when she was fourteen.

At a farm near L'Annonciation I stayed for a week with a family that had nineteen sons and two daughters, and they were *all at home*. I jokingly remarked to the mother one day, "If you were to lose one of these little boys I don't suppose you would ever miss him."

She was naturally highly indignant and put me in my

place by saying, "I love every one of them. They are all different and I would grieve if any one of them left me."

Religion was not the only encouragement to large families, of course. Although the French did tend to raise larger families than the English, it was the homesteading life that resulted in the huge families so characteristic of rural Canada at the turn of the century. In both the East and the West, our pioneering farmers had an immense amount of work to do, and dividing it up among a brood of boys and girls made it all that much easier — and probably a great deal more fun.

6 PRAIRIE
   RAILROADING

In March 1904, while I was still at L'Annonciation, a new assistant engineer in the person of Frank Paget arrived. The job was coming to an end and the engineering staff as well as the contractors had either departed or were making preparations for the next move. Railroaders will work almost anywhere there is work to be done. At that time the new transcontinental railway sponsored by the old Grand Trunk Railway and the federal government was attracting many of them. For many months a bitter controversy had raged in Parliament and in the press about the route to be taken. but now it was settled that it would run, from Quebec City to Winnipeg at least, far north of the Canadian Pacific main line. This second line later became the Canadian National Railway. It was difficult to get enough experienced engineers and contractors to do the work, so jobs were easy to find.

However, in spite of the lure of the new project in a new part of Canada, hitherto known only to the Indians and fur traders, Frank Paget and some other engineers thought that they could get to the Klondike goldfields more cheaply by travelling overland from Edmonton instead of taking the usual sea route up the Pacific coast to Skagway, and thence by foot and boat to Dawson City in the Yukon.

Their plan was to go to Edmonton by train, then to proceed via the Athabaska River and Great Slave Lake, on to the mighty Mackenzie River which flowed north. At a suitable point they would travel west over the mountains to the headwaters of the Yukon River and float down to Dawson. They were all men well experienced in wilderness travel, used to walking long distances over rough country and practised in the use of a canoe. They hoped to accomplish the journey before winter set in. I was asked to join the party and was eager to go.

Thank Heaven we gave up the idea when we heard stories of men who had attempted and failed. We had greatly underestimated the perils and difficulties of the proposed expedition.

In April, just as I was closing up my books and wondering where I was going next, Frank Paget got a letter telling him to send me to Montreal by the next train. I was to report at once to the stores department at the Hochelaga shops as the general storekeeper wanted to see me.

The stores department of the railway kept practically

everything that a railway used except food and stationery; in addition, it operated locomotive and car shops, where it manufactured most of its own rolling stock. The purchasing agent bought what the shops did not make and most of the purchases went into stores, where they were available on demand to any division or else sent directly to the job.

Hundreds of men worked in the Hochelaga shops, named after an ancient Indian village that was located near this area when the French first arrived in 1635. In modern Montreal that meant Ste. Catherine Street East, but about a year after I first saw them they moved to the brand new and modern Angus shops in the northeast end of Montreal.

The general storekeeper at this time was Mr. W. H. Kelson, whom I had known since my boyhood as our families were friends and I had played with his youngest son Laurie. There were three sons and one daughter in the family, all of whom I liked and all very fine people, but Mr. Kelson was a tyrant at the shops. He was born in England and came to the CPR in 1882 as general storekeeper at Winnipeg while the road was still under construction. Only three years later he was moved to Montreal to become general storekeeper of the whole system, a position he held until he resigned in 1904. He must have been highly regarded by the company's directors to have held this post so long.

It was a good thing that I knew him because he couldn't scare me as he would a stranger. He had one method of cutting people down before he interviewed them, and that was to keep them waiting. I had been told to report by *first train*, but now he kept me waiting in the outer office, sitting on a high, old-fashioned bookkeeper's stool with nothing to do, *for three days*. Then, on the third evening he called me in at about ten minutes to six and told me that I was to go to Regina, District of Assiniboia,

Northwest Territories, that night on No. 1. He handed me a pass and told me that I was to report to Mr. Barker at the railyard. Barker was a little Englishman who looked something like Rudyard Kipling and had spent most of his adult life in the Argentine. He knew nothing about Canada, railways or rails.

Mr. Kelson asked me if I had any questions and I said, "Yes, I have no money. I have not yet received my pay for March nor reimbursement for my expense account." Mr. Kelson called in Stewart, his chief clerk and a fine fellow, and told him to give me a cheque for sixty dollars on account. When I returned to the outer office Stewart told me that my salary had been raised from forty to sixty dollars a month, authorized, without a doubt, by Mr. Kelson. I slept that night on the comfortable train and thoroughly enjoyed the next two or three days with its new scenery and excellent food.

Most of the country west of Ottawa to Winnipeg consisted of woodland, lakes and rivers, but my first sight of the prairies came as we pulled into Winnipeg. They were just starting to build what became the famous Royal Alexandra Hotel, named after our Queen, the spouse of King Edward VII. I stayed over for one train so that I could have a look at the city I had heard about so often. There was nothing much to see, but I walked along Main Street to the corner of Portage, then west on Portage until there was nothing at all to see but unlimited acres of heavy mud, the rich black soil which produces the world-famous Manitoba No. 1 hard wheat.

The next morning we pulled into Regina, soon to be the capital of the new province of Saskatchewan but then an untidy-looking, badly laid-out town of less than five thousand people, with no pavements and traversed by tree-less streets that were, in the spring of 1904, canals of heavy mud and water. The scene I remember is in great contrast to the present attractive city with its Parliament Buildings reflected in Lake Wascana and its pleasing homes, trees and parks. However, I had no time to explore the town as I had to find Parker and report to him. I went to the station agent as a fellow employee of the CPR and found that Barker was located at the railyard one mile east of town, where the grade for the new branch line had been built to Arcola, ninety miles southeast in a line as straight as an arrow, the longest tangent in Canada. No transport was available, so I had to lug my suitcase containing all my earthly possessions down the main-line track to where I saw a string of boxcars and piles of rusty rails. This was the yard, evidently. I could see that it was flooded at least eighteen inches deep with muddy water. The rail piles were half submerged and rusty and the only dry footing was the centre of the track. I inquired of the first man I met which was Mr. Barker's car; he pointed it out and I wallowed my way over to it in my one good suit.

I climbed the few steps to the side door, knocked and walked in.

Mr. Barker was a short, near-sighted man who wore heavy glasses. He was seated at a table, writing. We recognized each other and shook hands but without any cordiality as we had taken a dislike to each other on sight. A small cubbyhole had been partitioned off at each end of the car; one a bunk and the other a wooden box for a dresser. The rest of the car was one general-purpose room with the standard CPR pot-bellied coal heater in the centre. He had allowed the fire to go out, which annoyed me because I was wet and cold.

I must explain that at this time, the building of heavier locomotives and cars had made it mandatory that rails should be made heavier. A coast-to-coast programme was being put into effect by which the light 56-pound and 60-pound rails, made in England were being torn up and relaid on branch lines and sidings; they were replaced on the main line with the much heavier and longer 80-pound steel. The weight of rails is calculated by each yard of length. Rails are now 39 instead of 33 feet long and are welded together in continuous lengths of 1440 feet instead of being bolted together one at a time. Weight has increased from 80 pounds per yard to 100 pounds in most regions, and even up to 150 pounds on main lines where the traffic is heaviest. What was going on here was that we got the discards from some division east of us, and they were in poor shape. Rails that had been curved when picked up were still bent; rails were often worn more on one side than the other, while there were many that had battered ends. All this from twenty years of traffic. What we had to do was make the crooked straight, saw off the battered ends and bore new bolt holes, all by hand. No power tools in those days. Moreover, the Doukhobors who made up our gang of about thirty men had to do this work while standing in a foot or two of cold water.

The Doukhobors were members of a religious sect that came from Russia to avoid military service. They operated as a community with a head man whose word was law. They gave the authorities a great deal of trouble with their marches across the country, but they were excellent workmen and we got along well together. No doubt they were homesick in a strange land; few spoke any English but they had one link with home. Every morning at about 10 o'clock the CPR's crack passenger train, No. 1, appeared in the far distance. Standing on a rail pile they watched as it grew larger and larger. Then, when it was directly opposite us, it gave a long blow on its bull-throated whistle and the Douks as one man would stop and say "Number One", which was about all the English they knew. The graceful train with its long locomotive and short smokestack followed by about thirteen slick coaches glided past us. It was a link with home and it always pleased them. I must confess that I got a kick out of it too.

We put the curved rails through a railbending machine in reverse to straighten them. The rails that had been treated were then piled separately, ready for the end of steel, or the "front", as it was often called. Each day we had to repair enough rails to make up a trainload of ten or twelve cars. In the evening we could see the train coming back from the end of steel; in fact, because the country was so flat and the air so clear, we could see the smoke for at least two hours before the train came in. The locomotive would go into the Regina yards, get turned around on a big turntable, take on coal and water and come back to us to haul rails and ties to the front.

The previous winter had been a hard one with more than the usual amount of snow, so that when it melted the plains were flooded. A bridge between Regina and Saskatoon had been washed out and hundreds of immigrants destined for the Saskatoon area were held at Regina until the bridge was repaired. These people were central Europeans: Rumanians, Ukrainians from Russia, Poles and Germans. For the most part they wore the familiar leather, sheepskin-lined coats. The CPR had to put up tents for them near the station and supplied cooking and sanitary facilities.

We boarded with the contractor's staff in their dining car where the food was good and plentiful.

The nearest potable water to be had was at the CPR well near the station, a mile distant. The water pump was operated by a windmill and there was seldom a time when the wind wasn't blowing. One of us would go and get a pailful once a day. When it was poured out it fizzed like ginger ale because of the alkali. There was always a long queue of immigrants with pots and pails waiting their turn.

The citizens of Regina were put on short rations because of the water shortage. Water was available for only ten minutes on the clock hour. People used to set their alarm clocks to go off at the hour. Sometimes the pressure was insufficient to supply water to the second storey.

One day after I had been uptown I was returning by the only serviceable path, which was the railway track. The ditches alongside were deep in water. As I walked the ties, I saw ahead of me in the water ditch a nude woman, one of the immigrants, having a bath. There was nowhere I could hide so I kept on; as I came abreast of her she looked up and smiled, as much as to say, "What else can I do?" Things were kind of primitive in Regina in those days.

On another shopping expedition I saw a tall Cree Indian striding along in moccasins, his black hair in two braids down the front and his squaw following him, carrying a papoose in a board carrier on her back. He was a tall, handsome man, but sad-looking as most Indians are, and no wonder with their old life as buffalo hunters gone forever. A little farther along I saw a cowhand complete with fringed chaps and wide frontier hat ride his horse up the steps to the side door of the Windsor Hotel, push the swinging door open, ride up to the bar and have a drink, pay for it and depart, without ever dismounting.

Another time I watched a teamster with two horses try to pull an empty Bain wagon out of the mud on Regina's main street, without success. At every shop entrance there were anything from one to six footscrapers, and everyone, men and women, wore rubber boots.

I had met a young man on the train named McCallum who told me that he was in the real estate business, so one day when I was passing McCallum & Hill's office I dropped in. He interested me in some vacant lots and I agreed to go out and look at them. He ordered a horse and buggy to come around; we drove west about four blocks past the last house in town and I bought two twenty-five-foot lots on Retallack Street, about five blocks from where the big CPR Hotel Saskatchewan stands today. After I returned to the East, I made the mistake of reconsidering my purchase; I decided that I had used poor judgement, and sold them for a modest profit.

One day a tall, red-headed Irishman named Rankin dropped in on us at the yard. I never knew just what his position was except that he was some kind of inspector who worked directly under Mr. Kelson; a kind of secret agent, I suspect. He found some fault with the way Barker was treating the rails and Barker denied it. I had warned Barker about this fault and now Rankin was on to it. I have forgotten the details, but in the argument Rankin called Barker a liar. After Rankin had left, Barker said to me, "What would you do if someone twice your size and half your age called you a liar?" I said, "There was nothing you could have done under the circumstances, but of course Rankin was right." Barker was incredulous, so I took him out into the yard and showed him what I had told him before. In my opinion, poor Barker's most outstanding characteristic was his all-round insufficiency.

I suppose we had a bad case of what lonely men call "cabin fever"; Barker and I carried on a continual feud about the fire and the housekeeping generally. However, the warmer weather soon solved the stove problem, and an order from Mr. Kelson soon separated me and the little Englishman. I never found out how he ended up, for orders came through for me to report to the storekeeper at the big yards at Fort William (now Thunder Bay). I was on the next train. When one worked for W. H. Kelson, the next train meant *the next train*, even if it left in half an hour.

7 RAILS

Fort William was like a second home to me. My father had been born there in 1855, the first white child to be born at the Fort, and his maiden sister, my Aunt Annie, was still living there with the Grahams, almost next door to Peter and John McKellar, the well known old-timers. However, I had to live close to my work so I got lodgings in a good home near the station. The boarders were all railway train or enginemen so I heard plenty of shop talk. I reported on arrival to Mr. W. W. Neeland, the storekeeper, who had an office beside the many miles of tracks that made up the yard and close to the grain elevators and the river. He was glad to see me because his inadequate but efficient staff had too much to do, and if I took over the rail end of his duties, he would be vastly relieved. Mr. Neeland was a fine old gentleman and it was a pleasure to work for him. All the time I was at the Fort I had only one small difference with Mr. Neeland, or rather with his boss in Montreal. There was a timeclock in his office and every employee was expected to punch it on entering and leaving, but I refused to do so. This was drawn to Mr. Neeland's attention by head office. My argument was that I worked overtime without any extra pay and that I should be trusted to do my job without punching any clock. The argument went on by mail with the Montreal office for a month, but I never punched the clock.

The Fort William yards were laid out to accommodate most of the grain traffic originating on the prairies. That means that they covered a very large acreage and contained many miles of tracks and dozens of switches. It was a fearsome place to walk through on a dark rainy night, as cars were constantly being switched silently and one had to keep alert. One dark night I was walking in the centre of the track with Mr. Neeland when I felt, rather than saw, a large shadow in front of us. I grabbed Neeland's arm and yanked him to one side as the tall black shape of a boxcar glided silently by, the result of a flying switch.

Near the waterfront there were five or six huge grain elevators and between the elevators and the waterfront docks ran a siding of two tracks to serve the elevators. We had the use of one of these tracks. At Port Arthur, now part of Thunder Bay, were huge grain elevators and extensive yards too.

It was in the Fort William yards that I got my first lesson in memory training.

One night I was standing on the long station platform near the yardmaster when a switchman came up to him and said "Where will I find car CP 234 678?" As I have said, the yards contained miles of tracks and the cars changed places every day, but the yardmaster said without hesitation, "Near the end on track 16."

Another time on this same platform I saw a freight conductor standing still and watching a long string of cars going slowly past. He never made a note but when the string had passed he took out a notebook and a pencil and wrote down all their numbers. He had literally photographed them on his brain. Some politicians have become famous for their ability to remember names. Railroaders were more interested in numbers.

I thought to myself, if he can do that, so can I, and I began to be more observant. First of all, I realized that all cars are classified. For instance, all boxcars ended with an even number; all flats with an odd number. Refrigerator cars always began with the figure 8 and so on. (This system has been changed as cars have been built for special purposes.) Then I began to classify them into other categories such as tonnage and length. After about a year of practice, I found that I could remember numbers better than names. If I had to check two flatcar loads of ties which came in no. 1 and no. 2 grades and it happened to be a very cold day and I didn't want to take off my mitts to write, I would leave the yard office and go out and mentally note down the car numbers and count the ties. I could then go back and sit down near the stove and make up the tally. I couldn't do it today, but it was useful then.

My job was simple but arduous. Steamships docked at our rail siding and unloaded their cargoes of new 80-pound steel rails made at the Algoma Steel Company mills at

Sault Ste. Marie, Ontario, generally known as the Soo. Cargo vessels of various sizes would dock opposite our siding, open their hatches, haul the rails up from the hold with steam derricks and swing them over the side. The rail gang would take the first two rails, lay them from the dock to the ship's rail and grease them. Then they would lay two more rails parallel but flat on the dock. On these the descending rails would be laid straight and even by means of heavy iron hooks. After one row was laid on its flanges, two rails were laid on top and the next row was built with the ball of the rail turned in to the spaces between the first rails. This made a good flat bed for the next row.

Rails came clattering down at a terrifying speed and clanged noisily into position as fast as the men could move. Each rail weighed 880 pounds. My job was to count them. Sometimes the ship would unload from two or three hatches at once; since we had to have a gang for each hatch, I had to hop from one to the other and keep track by marking the last rail with a piece of blue chalk.

Steamship captains the world over hate wasting time in harbour, so they will keep unloading all night. Our foreman would get a night gang on but I had no relief; I had to work right through until the ship was empty. Furthermore, while this unloading was going on, and sometimes from two ships at once, I had to keep track of the rails that were being loaded into boxcars. I had a shipping list and had to keep an eye on the quantity that went into each car so that it would not be overloaded, break down en route and cause a train wreck. What with checking the rails that were being unloaded off ship and then being loaded into cars and putting shipping cards on the boxcars, I could sympathize with the man who runs a three-ring circus.

One day, as I was very actively attending to my duties, a well-dressed stranger came walking towards me between the tracks.

"How many tons are you putting in that car?" he said abruptly.

I suspected that he was an officer of the company but when he did not introduce himself, I gave him an evasive answer because I thought I should not give this kind of information to a stranger.

He walked on without further words but the foreman, who had been eyeing me, came over and said,

"Do you know who that was?"

"No."

"That's G. J. Bury, general superintendent."

"Well, why couldn't he have said so?"

I thought he might report me to Neeland for incivility or lack of co-operation, but I must have said the right thing because Neeland told me later that the incident had not been mentioned.

Mr. Bury must have been a man of considerable ability. He started as a clerk in the purchasing department and rose through successive ranks in the service from North Bay to the Rocky Mountains until he became one of the vice-presidents of the company.

Of course there were times when no ships were in port, and then we all got a breather. It was pleasant by the riverside where there was always a breeze.

On the social side I had an enjoyable time. Mrs. Graham opened the season by inviting me to lunch one Sunday when I was free. Mrs. Peter McKellar was there. Then she arranged a meeting with the two Smellie girls, Beth and Pearl. They were the daughters of the well-known Dr. Smellie who owned the drugstore. A perfect name for a drugstore, he used to say. The two girls were tall and lovely, and they and Mrs. Smellie made life very pleasant for me during the six weeks I was there. Pearl later became matron-in-chief of the Canadian Army in the Second World War.

I had often gone out in a canoe at night with other young people when the lake was calm. No other time was advisable, for the wind can whip up a sea on Lake Superior, and waves that would not disgrace the Atlantic.

We used to float quietly there, sometimes singing, always watching the lights of the twin cities of Fort William and Port Arthur (now known as Thunder Bay), and we were occasionally rewarded by the sight, in the far distance, of the headlight of a locomotive hauling the Imperial Limited on its way to the Pacific. The light seemed to swivel from right to left as it lit up the sides of the deep rock cuts and the nearby hillsides, or flashed over the water of the lake as it followed the weaving and twisting roadbed close to the shoreline.

When it got close to Port Arthur, we would see a burst of white steam shoot silently upward from the engine's centre, but about a minute later we would hear clearly across the water the deep tones of the whistle; two long blasts followed by one short and one long, the signal for a crossing.

There is no sound like it today.

One night No. 1, the Imperial Limited, which carried the mail, was late. The lost time had to be made up so the best engine in the roundhouse, the 808, was run out and coupled on during the twenty-minute stop. Arthur, the fireman called for the run, was well known in our boarding house although I had never met him. His friends on board knew that he would have to shovel at least fifteen tons of coal into the roaring fire hole under the boiler during the length of his run over the subdivision of 120 miles. They probably were travelling too fast in order to make up time and, at a bridge near Wabigoon, the engine jumped the track and fell into the river. Both men of the engine crew were drowned. There was gloom in our house when the news arrived, for Arthur was highly regarded amongst the "eagle eyes" and those who swung a scoop shovel.

One of our boarders wrote a poem about the incident which I have long since lost; but I remember the first few lines:

The mail was late
and the eight O eight
came out to run it through, . . .

The men who drive and run our trains are specialists and they have a fine sense of brotherhood.

It was not customary in those days for the company to give holidays with pay, but I had wangled a week's leave and planned to join a party of about a dozen who were sailing out to the famous Silver Islet in Lake Superior to camp there for a week. We were to start on a Sunday, but I got one of Mr. Kelson's laconic telegrams, saying REPORT FIRST TRAIN MONTREAL. My holiday went out the window.

The first train left in twenty minutes and I knew I had better be on board. I made a hurried call to Aunt Annie, telling her to spread the news. Then I ran to the nearby station.

Two mornings later I walked in to W. H. K.'s office about 9 a.m. He ignored me and went on reading his paper, which he held right in front of his face. This was standard procedure and was designed to reduce the moral of employees, but I knew him too well to be impressed. He put the paper down, looked at me and said, "When did you get in?"

"This morning, sir."

"Did you get my wire to stop off at Sudbury?"

"No, sir."

For once someone had moved faster than he thought possible.

"Well, go back to Sudbury tonight. Mr. Stewart will tell you what to do."

He raised his paper before his face as a sign of dismissal.

Stewart told me that I had to go back to Sudbury, a mere three hundred miles, on the NEXT TRAIN and take a pair of angle irons with me to see if they fitted some twenty miles of old rails piled in the Sudbury yards. Of course the section foreman at Sudbury could have done it just as well. The angle irons could have been sent to him by baggage car and he could have wired the result. However, it suited W. H. K. to move people around on sudden notice.

I lugged those heavy irons on a hot Sunday from the Sudbury station to the rail pile some distance down the Soo Line and lugged them back to the station, where I waited for hours for an eastbound train. The irons did not fit.

On my return, I was put to work at a high desk out at the Angus shops and given the job of keeping track of all the rail movements on the CPR from coast to coast. Carpenters were laying a new wood floor on the concrete base of the new office and the noise was deafening. Every division superintendent on the whole system had to wire the general storekeeper every morning how many and what kind of rails he had received on the previous days, how many miles he had laid, how many tons he had shipped out and to whom, together with car numbers. These wires were passed on to me.

I simply couldn't cope with it alone and asked Stewart for help. In a day or two a nice old gentleman reported to me. Judging by his clothing and manners he had seen better days, but he was of little help to me as he didn't know a rail from a bamboo fishing pole. However, I got what mileage I could out of him without blowing my top and he was kind enough to invite me out to his lakeshore cottage one evening for supper and a sail on the lake.

One day Mr. Baker, one of the road's vice-presidents, phoned W. H. K. and wanted a list, in detail, of all the rails between Halifax and Vancouver that were piled in storage. This request was handed to me. I worked nights and finally came up with a list; after it had been submitted I lay awake that night doing arithmetic in my head and then I remembered — I had forgotten to include those orphan twenty miles of steel in the Sudbury yard. I decided to let it ride.

The West was filling up quickly and branch lines were being built as fast as three railways could get charters, and materials and men to lay them down.

As stations were located about every eight miles, a great deal of ingenuity was called for in naming new townsites. Sometimes the physical setting provided inspiration, as in Elbow and Outlook. In the period after the South African War, several villages took their names from heroes and events in that conflict: Baden, Powell, Mafeking, Redvers, Smuts and Wauchope. It was an era that glorified patriotism, empire and the stiff upper lip, as demonstrated on the Kerrobert-Lacombe branch where we find this lineup: Onward, Superb, Major, Fusilier, Compeer, Monitor, Consort, Loyalist, Veteran, Throne, Coronation, Fleet. On the Regina-Young line, Holdfast, Liberty, Stalwart, Imperial and Amazon are similarly inspired. Young itself is the fourth of a quintet named in alphabetical order, which also includes Undora, Watrous, Xena, and Zelma. One of these branches was a line starting at Kirkella in Manitoba near the Saskatchewan border and running northwest to Saskatoon. At the time I am speaking of, it had reached Lipton, a little northeast of Regina, and there a material yard had been established.

I was suddenly sent out there to organize the rail-yard. Taking the NEXT TRAIN, I travelled to Winnipeg on No. 1. Then I caught a local to Kirkella, but found out at the hotel that there would be no train to the front until morning, when a mixed passenger and freight would go as far as Tantallon, fifty miles up the line. I took this and learned on arrival that the next hundred miles was still under the construction department and there was no way to get up except by a locomotive that would come down the following morning from the end of steel, or 'the front' as it was usually called, to get its boiler washed out at Tantallon where there was a water tank and plenty of water in the Qu'Appelle River. I said to the agent,

"What's your name?"

"Paynter."

"The only Paynter I ever heard of was a man who owned a beach on the Georgian Bay near Owen Sound at a place called Paynter's Bay. We used to picnic there."

"That was my father."

He said that there was no hotel yet but that they expected to have one soon. I asked if I could sleep on the bench in the waiting room. He assented but told me that it was against rules to allow anyone to stay in the station after he had locked up and not to talk about it.

I had a fretful sleep without blankets and got up early from my hard couch. For the sake of something to do I went down to the river bank, stripped off my clothes and dived in, without testing the temperature of the water with my toes. I gasped when I surfaced, for the water was the coldest I had ever experienced except for the time I fell through the ice at Labelle. I ran up and down the bank to restore my circulation; then I dressed and went up to the

102

main street to look for some place to eat, and was very glad to find a Chinese restaurant open. Never did a bowl of hot oatmeal porridge taste so good.

The locomotive came but it was several hours getting washed out. As we finally prepared to leave, the fireman kindly gave me his seat on the left side, explaining that he would never get a chance to sit down as he would be busy firing coal. A locomotive is about the dirtiest and most uncomfortable vehicle I know for a ride, so I was thoroughly begrimed by the time I reached Lipton. My suit was fit only for the cleaners and my face was like the fireman's—black.

I stayed there a month, in lovely Saskatchewan fall weather.

One day there was a yell for help and I saw smoke near the cookhouse. I took the rail gang and ran over. The cook had thrown some hot ashes, against all orders, into a woodbox near the kitchen door. The wind had fanned it into flame and the fire was now running west through the prairie grass which was then as dry as tinder. The wind was blowing it straight for Lipton. All hands turned out and we fought that fire all afternoon. The cook and his cookees supplied pails of water, sacking and bags which we tried to keep wet, and used to beat the fire out; we would just get it under control when it would break out somewhere else. In the end, though, our efforts were successful and the fire was put out.

On a quiet day when the yard was closed down I thought I would walk over to Fort Qu'Appelle, a famous place in the 1880s, located in the Qu'Appelle Valley, about twelve miles distant. It was a beautiful day in September, the West's loveliest month I always think. I had not had any mail for weeks and thought that some might have been addressed to the fort. But there was no mail, so I had lunch at the hotel and walked back. On the way I was met by a mounted policeman, a young Englishman, and I guessed he was just beginning service. We chatted a while and then he asked me how far it was to the fort. I was surprised as I thought that the Mounties knew everything about the country — he must have been a very new recruit. I thought the country lovely with its scattered bluffs of little trees and its occasional sloughs. The air was full of wild ducks and the bluffs usually had some prairie chicken. I didn't see one house on the way.

The fireman, Frank, who had given me his seat on the way to Lipton, came to me one evening and suggested that we go duck hunting. Wild ducks were all about us — every slough held a small flock. Frank had borrowed a shotgun from the cook and I thought he knew what he was about, so I trailed along, just as a spectator though, as I knew nothing of duck shooting. We were not sportsmen out to shoot birds on the wing; we were hunting for the pot in order to get a change of diet from beef and pork.

We came to one of the natural ponds that dotted the countryside and saw five or six ducks swimming around. On the far side was a homesteader's soddy and we could see a man and some kids moving about, doing various chores.

The fireman crept through the long grass that bordered the pond; then, near the edge, he knelt down in the mud, took careful aim and fired.

All the birds took flight except one which was wounded and could only flap about feebly, so Frank took off his boots and socks, rolled up his overalls and waded out to capture his prize. At the same time, all of the farmer's family strolled down to the water'e edge on the far side to watch the fun. After some awkward floundering in the deep mud under the water, my pal made a great diving lunge at the unfortunate bird and managed to grab it by one leg, but in doing so he fell flat on his face in the mire.

As he came up, plastered with mud and with water dripping from his face, but still hanging on to the duck's leg, he faced the farmer.

"What's the idea of shooting my ducks!" the homesteader asked mildly.

"Your ducks! Why these are wild ducks and anybody can shoot them."

"Oh, no. These are part of my domestic stock and that one there (indicating the nearly dead duck) will cost you fifty cents."

Frank's fingers were too muddy and his pants too wet to dig into his pockets, so I walked around the end of the pond and paid the fine. Still, we had duck for dinner.

8 THE TORONTO-SUDBURY BRANCH

A day or two later I got the usual abrupt wire to report to Montreal at once.

Again I was caught away from home without money, as I had been moving around and the payroll had not caught up to me. However, I boarded a work train which fortunately for me ran all the way to Kirkella. Then I waited for the first eastbound regular passenger train on the main line. I had no authority except the telegram, so when the conductor came along asking for tickets I had to tell him I had none and relate my improbable story. I could imagine what was going on in his mind: "Should I put this young hiker off at the next station or let him ride for free?" He never knew when a "spotter" might be on board counting the passengers. He looked dubious, so, on impulse, I asked him his name.

"Macintyre," he answered, to my delight. Here was a clansman! I worked on that angle and he carried me free to Winnipeg.

Arriving at Winnipeg, I went straight to the office of G. J. Bury, general superintendent of the central division. His chief clerk, D. C. Coleman, took my story into his boss and, after some argument in which Bury wanted to know what in hell I was doing out here anyway in his territory without him being notified, he finally told Coleman to give me a pass to Montreal. So far so good, but I wasn't finished.

"I have no money to pay for berth and meals," I said. "Could you advance me twenty-five dollars or cash one of my personal cheques?" Bury snorted but told Coleman to do it. I am glad to say that Coleman eventually became president of the CPR. He was a winner and I should have got a job with him.

About two nights after I returned to Montreal and looked with distaste at that rail desk, Frank Paget, the engineer with whom I had worked as clerk at L'Annonciation, phoned me at home. He said that he was at the Queen's Hotel and would like to see me.

I went right down and found Frank in his room. After the usual preliminaries he said, "I am in charge of the construction of the north end of the Toronto-Sudbury line and live at Wanapetei about twelve miles east of Sudbury. I have a material clerk but he is unsatisfactory. I can get rid of him and would like you to take his place. The salary will be eighty dollars a month instead of the sixty you are now getting. I want you to come and I can arrange it."

I liked working for Frank and I told him I would be glad to go. I went in to the office the following morning and told Stewart of my decision. I was leaving him in a bit of a hole as far as rails were concerned, so he said, "I wish you wouldn't go. You are doing well here and you will go far." I told him I was sorry to leave him short-handed but that I couldn't stick it any longer in the office. Within twenty-four hours my transfer was arranged and I got a letter from F. S. Darling, division engineer, enclosing a pass to Wanapetei and telling me to go at once as the general storekeeper had been informed. I was delighted to be freed from that desk job, but I had learned a lot about rails during the past few years. I could tell the weight of any rail simply by feeling its ball with my hand, and I knew any type of freight car by its number.

I arrived at Wanapetei in daylight and found my sleeping car and office car, which were converted boxcars, on a siding right opposite the station which in turn was on a curve. In every boxcar there is a small window at each end and a wide door at each side. My bunk was at one end near the small window. I was tired, went to bed early and soon fell asleep. In the middle of the night I had what I thought was a nightmare; my room was flooded with a bright light that approached me along with a roar that grew louder with every second. Then, just as I thought I was to be engulfed in some horrible catastrophe, a fearful shriek sounded right beside me. I landed on the floor prepared to run for my life . . . and then the long string of freight cars rushed by. It had been the locomotive, only four or five feet distant, whistling for the bridge. I curtained the window with something the next day, but from then on I never heard the engine's whistle.

The general contractors were Foley Bros. and Larsen

of Minneapolis, who had big American connections. Their office was in a temporary building across the Wanapetei River, a typical northern stream flowing south from Wanapetei Lake. There was no settlement between us and Hudson's Bay. It was now midwinter and the river was frozen, so we used it to cross on the ice to Foley's mess where we boarded. They had a good man as cook and gave liberal meals with plenty of variety.

Much lumbering was going on all along the Wanapetei but the village was quiet now as all the activity was in the woods. When the ice went out in April and the drive hit town, it would be lively enough.

I had a companion in the sleeping car, a fair-haired Swede with a beard named Olaf Swanson who claimed that he had worked on the Arctic Circle Railway in Norway. He was our draftsman and made up the plans and profiles as the information flowed in from our five line camps. Later we had posted to us an experienced bridge engineer, a German named Forenhofer, a man of considerable experience. He went back, I heard, to Germany in 1914 to fight for his fatherland.

We were on the northernmost section of the new line, that is, sixty miles from Byng Inlet on Georgian Bay to Sudbury, and the country was about as rough as any outside the mountains. The hills were not high but they were all solid rock, and criss-crossed with streams and lakes — ideal hunting and fishing country, since nobody lived in it except a few Indians.

There were no real roads, so that all travel in the summer was by canoe or by walking on forest trails, and in winter by dogsled or snowshoe. Walking is easier in winter than in summer; the snow fills the hollows and covers low bushes, small rocks and fallen logs, while the smooth frozen surface of lakes and rivers is best of all.

This particular line was being built to extend the CPR's service to central Ontario. For many years the only route to the new West possessed by the CPR was from Montreal. The lucrative traffic from central Ontario, with all its factories, cities, towns and farms making everything from canned goods to threshing machines, had to be shipped over the Grand Trunk Railway which had been established there for many years, but had no western lines. Freight and passengers were assembled in Toronto and then shipped via Barrie to North Bay, where they were transferred to the CPR for the journey west as far as Vancouver. Mr. W. F. Tye, chief engineer for the CPR, aptly called the G.T.R. line, a "series of toboggan slides". This situation had irked CPR directors for a long time so they decided to build a line of their own, a better and a shorter one and, while they were at it, one with easier curves and grades. This was to be known as the Toronto-Sudbury branch and would run from Bolton just west of Toronto to a point on the CPR's main line about seven miles east of Sudbury, a line 235 miles long. Modern engineers will be surprised to learn that this line with all its heavy rock and bridge work cost only a little less than eleven million dollars, the price of four hundred modern homes today.

I had not been there many weeks before Frank thought I should take a trip over the line with him in order to obtain a first-hand impression and meet the various engineers and their staffs. On most occasions Frank would travel with Pete Levesque by dogsled, but Pete was away on his weekly mail trip so we made the journey on snowshoes. Except at the rapids, the rivers and the lakes were frozen, so the going was level and easy. We did twenty miles each day.

There were five camps, each about ten miles apart and all on some part of the waterway. They had good substantial buildings constructed of whole logs properly chinked with moss or clay, or both. Each party consisted of the resident engineer, an instrument man, rodman and two chainmen as well as a cook. They obtained their food supplies from the contractor's stores.

The first camp was at some rapids near the big Baby Lake cut. A young engineer was the resident and he had the rock section. Here was the deepest rock cut I ever saw: 102 feet deep and said to be deeper than anything in the Rockies. In the mountains such an obstacle would have been tunnelled, but here the engineers deliberately threw the line into the rock in order to get fill for the long embankment they needed on both sides. Standing at the top of this little mountain and looking straight down its almost perpendicular face on a sunny summer day, one could see a tiny patch of jewel-like turquoise blue. This was Baby Lake.

Before the short winter day ended, we pushed on to Elbow Lake where Macready was in charge, and where we had supper and slept. The country from there on was fairly level and heavily forested, but the trails had been pretty well broken so we reached Fred Rutter's camp in time for lunch. Frank thought that we could make Hay's camp on Pakeshkeg Lake by dark.

The snow was deep and the going heavier so that it was dark by the time we reached the Pickerel River. The Pickerel runs parallel to the French, but the French was the larger stream and was the historic route of the old fur traders between Lake Nipissing and the Georgian Bay. I could not help thinking that my grandparents, John and Jane McIntyre with baby Mary, had travelled this way in 1849 on their way up to Lake Superior and then on to Lake Brunswick, the Hudson's Bay Company fort halfway to James Bay.

We heard wolves howling when we were halfway across. Some people say that wolves never attack a man, but the howls got closer and I hated to cross the open spaces made by the two rivers where there were no trees to climb. As we crossed the wide French the wolves seemed closer and we carried no firearms. At last we reached shore and after a short trek through the woods came to Hay's camp at Pakeshkeg Lake.

Both these rivers had to be bridged and winter was a good time to make the surveys, when the engineers could walk on the ice.

We slept there and the next day reached Isbester's camp at Byng Inlet, where the Magnetawan River empties into Georgian Bay, in time for lunch. Isbester was a big, self-confident fellow of considerable experience in whom Frank placed a good deal of confidence.

I should say that Frank and I had taken much more than a cross-country stroll, because he inspected all important work with his residents as he went along. On returning to Wanapetei we followed our own trail, and as we passed through each camp gave us mail "for the outside".

During that winter the Honourable Francis Cochrane, minister of Lands and Mines for Ontario and some years later minister of Railways and Canals in the federal government, used to arrange to have his train stop for a few minutes at Wanapetei and by appointment have a chat with Frank Paget. He was naturally interested in the new rail line that would serve his constituency of Nipissing East and the town of Sudbury where he had been mayor several times.

On a cold, below-zero winter day, Mr. Cochrane made one of his infrequent visits. The steam escaping from the heating pipes made a cloud of vapour between the cars. After a brief talk Mr Cochrane shook hands in parting with Frank, stepped back into the cloud of steam to board his

112

train and was lost to our view. We stood there waiting for the train to pass so that we could cross the tracks. Mr. Cochrane's private car was on the tail end as usual; as it passed, we all saw at once his fine otterskin cap lying between the rails.

Paget grasped the situation instantly and shouted to a trainman on the rear platform, "Stop that train!" The train was just beginning to move slowly but the trainman, without asking questions, immediately jerked the emergency bellcord and the engineer stopped within a few feet. We ran forward and found Mr. Cochrane hanging between the two cars with his hands on the chains of his own car but with one foot caught under the wheel of the car. He had stepped between the cars of course, blinded by steam. The trainman signalled the fireman to back up slowly and we got the minister out and on to the station platform, gave him what first aid the train crew had and wired Sudbury to have an ambulance ready. Later the leg was amputated. Everybody thought that the victim had shown rare courage and presence of mind. Mr. Cochrane lived and served his country for thirteen years after that — the town of Cochrane is named after him.

There was one awful row the following summer.

While Paget was away at Byng Inlet, one of the resident engineers and a few of his party came up to Wanapetei in canoes and persuaded two or three sporting girls to come back to camp with them. All might have gone well, but one canoe upset in a little rapids near Baby Lake just before reaching camp, and the girls in their long skirts were dumped in the swift water. There was quite a struggle and the boys did well to get all the girls to shore.

Frank returned to base the same day, thoroughly tired after his hard journey of 120 miles. He had not been home half an hour when somebody told him about the episode.

Fatigued as he was, he got into his canoe, paddled down to the camp and walked in on his men while the female clothing was still hanging out to dry where all could see it. He had caught them red-handed and promptly fired the whole party, giving them twenty-four hours to pack up and clear out.

The cut at Baby Lake was finished at last. It took something like fourteen months to complete, and it cost the lives of seven men.

There was an old foreman on this rock cut who would have been called an amputation case in the army and been put in a home for senior citizens with nurses to care for him. But this old veteran refused to quit. I was at his camp one night and watched him retire. It was quite a performance.

First he would remove his glass eye and hang it on the wall; then he would unstrap his right leg at the knee and stand it beside his bed where it would be within easy reach in case he had to run from a fire. After that he unbuckled his left arm and put it on a shelf beside him, and finally he would drop his dentures into a glass of water.

Although I lived at Wanapetei, because of its telegraph line, post office and boarding facilities, my main job was at a siding called Romford, five miles west, where we had put in a large material yard because this was where the new branch joined the main line from Montreal. There was nothing at Romford except the siding and our warehouse. For the first few weeks I had to walk the ties for five miles there and back; then I applied for a track velocipede, which saved a great deal of time. Like an ordinary velocipede it had two wheels, a low seat and a pair of handlebars. It was kept upright and on the track by a third wheel to the far rail. It was propelled by working a strong stick back and forth with the handlebars, while the feet remained stationary on rests. I could work up a fair turn of speed, but the rattling noise made it impossible to hear anything else.

At that time the CPR main line was single-tracked and the rider could only look forward. It was winter and the snowplough had left banks of snow along each side of the rails. As I rode along one day, I heard a roar behind me; looking round, I saw a huge 1600-class locomotive bearing down on me with steam spouting from its whistle and with both engineer and fireman leaning out their respective windows. I stopped and whipped the bike off the rails so as to clear the train.

The long freight roared by and the fireman yelled something at me which I could not hear. The wind caused by the train made such a cloud of snow powder that I turned my back on it and looked forward towards the engine and saw the fireman hanging out the window until the train went into a curve. Then, as the engine whistled a series of short blasts, the last boxcar came into view and I thought, "Just the van now and I can step back on the track." But as the front steps of the van drew opposite me, I saw a brakeman leaning away out and frantically signalling to me to get clear. I turned my head quickly and saw that the van was *not* the last car; behind it there was a flanger, a car with a long blade, or flange, sticking out at right angles, its purpose being to widen the snow bank on which I was lying ... and I was right in its path!

I did a quick back somersault over the bank and rolled away to safety, but the flanger picked up my bike and tumbled it in a wave of snow over the bank as well. "So that's why the engine whistled," I thought. To tell the train crew there was danger. I certainly owed my life to that quick-acting rear-end brakeman, and to the fireman.

I was unhurt and managed to dig myself out of the deep snow; then I crawled over the bike which, strangely enough, seemed undamaged. The snow had acted as a cushion. That night I asked the section foreman to get it back on the rails and bring it in.

One night in the spring I was awakened by the roar of a train rushing by my sleeping car. I looked out of the little window and saw a train of flatcars loaded with heavy timbers, ties, rails, a derrick and tools, followed by several boarding cars full of men from the bridge and building branch.

A few hours later another train, similarly equipped rushed by whistling shrilly in the night air. I saw a light in the station window opposite, so I slipped on some clothes and walked across the track. Watmough, the agent, was at the telegraph key. As soon as there was a pause I asked, "Where was the wreck?"

"It's not a wreck. It's a trestle on the Lake Superior division, burned down, and they're rushing every wrecking train we have between Fort William and North Bay. Passenger trains are stalled at both ends."

When the whistle blew the alarm signal at any roundhouse, members of the wrecking crew who were on duty dropped whatever they were doing and reported to the wrecking foreman. As there were no telephones in most homes, callboys jumped on their bicycles and pedalled to the homes or boarding houses of those off duty and probably asleep.

At every divisional point, cars of materials needed for repairs were kept ready loaded, so that trains were soon made up.

A man known as a "bank" fireman at the roundhouse started a fire under the boiler of the engine selected for the run. This was done by attaching a hose to a fitting on the smokebox of the locomotive, either from the shop boiler or from a high-pressure air tank, in order to make a draft.

Then the firebox was given a liberal layer of cotton waste soaked in kerosene and a light covering of coal. The fireman then ignited the whole mess by shovelling his flame thrower into it.

The coal soon ignited and more coal was added, but the external draft service was still required as the locomotive would not have sufficient steam to operate its own blower for nearly one and a half hours. While the boiler was getting hot, the regular engine crew would arrive, check over the essential parts and get their instructions from the locomotive foreman and/or, the assistant superintendent.

The opening between the engine and the tender was covered by a hinged iron plate so that the fireman would not fall between. He stood astride this plate, which slid back and forward with the engine's movements. He filled his big scoop shovel with soft coal, turned and, taking sure aim at the open door of the firebox, threw the coal in an expert scattering motion that ensured an even heat under the boiler. He opened and shut the firedoor by a chain suspended from the ceiling of the cab. He would shovel between ten and fifteen tons on a subdivisional run of about 120 miles depending on weather and track conditions.

On a fast emergency run like this he seldom had a chance to sit down, but from time to time he would look out along the left side for any signals; the engine driver watched on the right, controlling the locomotive with his throttle and brakes and handling the whistle, while the fireman rang the big brass bell by pulling on a light rope.

The train dispatcher back at the terminal knew where every train on the division was running or sidetracked, and so kept the main line clear for the wreckers.

It was a rough ride for those in the boarding cars, which were ordinary boxcars equipped with bunks. Usually there was at least one old passenger car included in the train.

The boxcars were fitted out with blankets, stoves and food, but without the superior springing that the passenger cars had as standard equipment.

Across the subdivision of 110 to 120 miles they sped, whistle shrieking for the crossings and way stations. At the end of the run another engine — watered, oiled and fueled and with steam up — would be waiting with a fresh crew, and in a few minutes they would be on their way.

The trestle was very high and very long and spanned a brawling stream swollen by melting snow. But the men worked at top speed and, through an incredible example of organization and well-trained co-ordination, they rebuilt the trestle in twenty-four hours.

I could imagine the scene. The main-line rails on both sides of the ravine would be cut and switches installed. Long sidings capable of holding two or three work trains would be laid. The main line would be kept free for arriving and departing trains. Later reports told of passengers on both sides climbing down one hillside and up the other, helped by workmen with their baggage. They could then board a train and continue their journey. I heard later that some stubborn, or elderly passengers refused to walk, claiming that they had paid their fares and were entitled to ride, so brawny railroaders carried them over! The railway mail clerks, feeling it was their responsibility, conveyed the mail sacks across.

In the summer of 1903, silver was discovered about fifty miles east of us.

There are many stories about how the discovery was made, but credit for the first claim must go to McKinley and Darragh who were the contractors for the T and NO Railway. They sent samples away and the assay showed very rich native silver. The following spring they erected a small plant. About six weeks later Fred Larose, a blacksmith working at his forge on the new railroad, was annoyed by an inquisitive fox and threw his smith's hammer at the animal. He missed, but struck a rock which exposed a rich vein of silver.

At any rate, the silver was found and with it, or nearby, valuable metal called cobalt. As soon as the news hit North Bay a rush of prospectors started; very quickly a camp was established, which grew into the town Cobalt. This was just the beginning of a whole series of discoveries in the territory north of Cobalt. Gold and copper were found in abundance, which meant that in a few years mines came into existence that became known to miners and investors everywhere. Mines like Hollinger, Dome, Noranda, Lakeshore, McIntyre and Kirkland Lake became some of the richest mines in the world. This was not like the Klondike of 1898, where a man with a pan and a shovel and a lot of guts could find gold dust in the streams of the country, and where miners from as far away as Australia and South Africa came to seek their fortunes. One had to have capital to develop these deep northern Ontario hard-rock mines. A poor prospector could find surface indications, strip the overburden off the rock and hire someone to drill test holes. But if it looked promising, a syndicate had to be formed or a big outfit with plenty of capital might be found who would buy it or take a majority interest.

Now all hard-rock men are prospectors at heart, and never go anywhere in rock country like the pre-Cambrian Shield without a miner's hammer with which to tap the rocks that look promising.

Hundreds left their jobs on our railway project and hundreds more came from Sudbury, where the big International Nickel Company's mine was located; then, as the news spread around the world, more came from all quarters. We saw them hanging on to the platforms of passenger cars and even sitting on the cowcatchers of the locomotives. Duncan and John McMartin, who were cousins, had a contract for part of the T and NO Railways; Duncan went into partnership with LaRose, whom he bought out later, and developed a very rich mine. The McMartins, often known as Red Jack and Black Jack, had a contract on the north end of our work. They also joined a very strong group that included the Timmins brothers, who developed the Hollinger mine.

I neglected to mention two other members of our party who were occasional visitors only. One was Joe Cole, an American who provided us with much entertainment. He had been in the American Navy and was a natural story-teller. He would keep us awake long after we should have closed our eyes telling us weird stories of his adventures, which we felt were largely fictional, but we could not resist listening to him. He always had an engaging smile and was a favourite with everyone. He was Paget's companion on canoe trips.

The other man was Pete Levesque, our French-Canadian mailman. Pete made a weekly trip over the line to Byng Inlet with the mail, in winter with his own dog team and sled and in summer by canoe. A modern *voyageur*.

As soon as the silver rush started to Cobalt in 1904, Joe Cole got restless and tried to persuade me to quit my job with the CPR and go with him to the new mining country. However, neither of us knew anything about this game, so Joe came up with the idea that we would open a hardware store. His argument was that everyone who came in would need hardware at once; picks and shovels, axes, dynamite, pots and pans, nails and so on. I was strongly tempted but thought that I had better speak to Frank first.

Frank had been through this kind of boom before in

B.C. His answer to me was: "Don't think of it. For every-one who makes any money up there, a hundred will go broke. Joe is a nice fellow but he is a wanderer and won't stay long there. He knows nothing about either mining or business. You are doing well with the company and will go further, so my advice to you is to stay here." I took his advice but Joe went, and I never heard of him again.

As for Pete, he approached me at the end of the summer and wanted me to spend the next winter in the bush with him, trapping. He thoroughly understood this craft and was already well equipped with an excellent team of dogs and a camping outfit. This was a more sensible proposition and the thought of such an experience while I was young strongly appealed to me, but ultimately I turned it down. The thought of spending six months in the bush with no companion but Pete, with nothing in common to talk about, nothing to read and no mail, no cash income and monotonous food, made me decide against it.

The work, except for the two big steel bridges over the Pickerel and the French, was pretty well finished on the north end by early fall. My job at Romford was also finished, as the yard was piled high with all the materials necessary for the northern section and the warehouse con-tained the articles that needed protection from the weather, such as finished lumber, sash and doors ready-glazed, paint, finishing hardware, nails and so on.

One day just before I left I went up to the yard to check on something. When I arrived I found that I had left my key at the office. The door was secured by a padlock and I thought that I could pry it off, so I looked around for a piece of iron to help me. Nearby was an upright wooden keg full of eighteen-inch boat spikes for a small wooden bridge, or culvert. As I took hold of one I noticed what I thought was clay at the bottom. I pulled the spike out and immediately I was attacked by what seemed to me to be thousands of very angry wasps. They made straight for me in a cloud and I ran for my life, halfway to Romford, a quarter of a mile away, before they gave up. I went back after regaining my breath but found them still buzzing around and very much annoyed, so I couldn't get near the door and had to go home.

The reason so many American engineers and contractors were employed by the railways at this time was that there were not enough trained and equipped people and firms in these categories in Canada to service the immense amount of work that was in progress, or planned for the immediate future, now that the CPR was pushing out branches in all directions and the Grand Trunk Pacific, the National Transcontinental and the Canadian Northern were all bridging the country from Montreal to the West Coast. In truth, the country was going through another rail-building phase even greater than the building of the Canadian Pacific in the 1880's. Our universities were not turning out engineers fast enough, so scores of men like chainmen and rodmen already on survey parties were taking courses with the international correspondence schools and the railways were accepting graduating certificates from these schools plus practical experience in the field (where they could learn a great deal from their own resident engineer) as sufficient qualification. An outstanding example of this practice was the boss engineer of the whole sixty miles of the Toronto-Sudbury line, Frank Paget, who had never gone to college.

The general contractors for this section were Foley Bros. and Larsen of Minneapolis. This Swedish-Irish-American company was a big outfit that was also in the wholesale grocery business. Their superintendent was a Swede named Swanson, who was a hustler.

One of the duties of resident engineers was to make up monthly estimates of the work done, which they did from the profiles they had made, and from these estimates the contractors were paid. All local profiles and estimates were sent to Paget and from these he had our draftsman, Swanson, make up a grand profile of the entire project. From it the total estimate for the month was calculated. Of course there were disputes from time to time between the contractor and the engineers about the quantities moved (for which the engineers were paid by the cubic yard) but the engineers' word was final. The main contractor sublet small sections to subcontractors and to station men. All these little station men were by contract obliged to purchase all their groceries, meat, hay and oats from the big contractor which was quite a racket as the prices charged were exorbitant. It is quite probable that the supply end of the contract was more profitable than the moving of earth and rock.

Towards the end of my term in the North, Mr. Swanson, Foley's walking boss, approached me with an offer to go with him to a big development they were about to open in Louisiana, where they proposed to log off a great tract of valuable timber, build a railway to get it out to market and, incidentally, build a new town.

He offered to double my present salary, which was tempting, but I did not consider it for a moment. I thought that I saw a bright future for Canada, and I loved my homeland too much to leave. There are more important things than money.

9 OLD ONTARIO

About the end of August I said goodbye to Frank and Mrs. Paget and the people at our boxcar headquarters and on order, travelled to Bolton Via Toronto and reported to Mr. E. T. Agate (spell it backwards, he said, it all comes out to the same thing). He was a long, loose-jointed Yankee from New England who chewed tobacco; Paget, who knew him, told me that he had the reputation of being the most sarcastic man on the CPR, but he was a competent engineer and was always very good to me.

I said that he was loose-jointed and he proved it once by standing in an open doorway and, with one foot on the floor, placing the sole of the other on the lintel above his head.

While I was up north we were never favoured with a visit from our division engineer, Mr. F. S. Darling, another Yankee, because he was a man who ran his division from his office and never came near the work in the field. For this reason he was unpopular with the personnel of the parties who made up ribald verses of a song about him, all derogatory, to the tune of an old war ditty called "He was only a volunteer", replacing the last word with "engineer".

However, in Bolton we were now only twenty miles from his office in Toronto and on the end of a telephone line. We could not boast the luxury of a phone so Agate had to walk to the drugstore every time Darling called and use the only public phone. Darling called almost daily, usually about something trivial such as the shortage of an axe on someone's monthly equipment report. Agate soon got tired of this and told him politely that next time he broke his lead pencil he would wire him.

The countryside from Bolton to Orillia was pleasant farmland dotted with apple orchards on which ripe apples now hung. All this was a great change from the rock and forest of northern Quebec and Ontario, with their forests of pine and spruce and cedar so different from the lovely maples, oaks and walnut trees of southern Ontario.

The people, too, were different, being nearly all of English, Scotch or German stock, living in good, well-maintained, prosperous communities. A little stream often wound its way through these small towns and villages, and sometimes this stream provided the power to run the local flour or grist mill.

To drive a railway through this orderly land did not

make the company popular, but the right-of-way agents employed by the company were very diplomatic and we had no real trouble. The old Grand Trunk Railway, however, delayed us at one point where we had to put in what is called a diamond crossing; that is, where one level track has to cross another. As we moved up with the ready-made rail crossing we found a GTR engine sitting on the site, whose engineer would not move without orders. This was very petty, as it had all been agreed upon months before, but some local official thought he was being clever. It took some telegrams and a few hours delay before we got the locomotive moved.

Bolton is on an old branch line to Owen Sound, so the twenty-mile gap between Bolton and Toronto was strengthened in anticipation of the longer trains and heavier rolling stock that would soon be passing over it. The Sudbury branch forked off the Owen Sound line about a mile west of Bolton, and we purchased a ten-acre field there for a material yard. To get to this property we had to cross a paltry fraction of an acre situated diagonally in the corner of a field. It was bordered on one side by a split-rail fence. We sent a train of a few cars up there and a gang to cut our wire fence and the farmer's wooden one, and then lay rails into our field, but when the gang got there they found an embattled farmer sitting on his fence, cradling a shotgun in his arms. He warned the gang that he would shoot the first man who set foot on his land.

Nobody on our side wanted a shooting war, so the railroaders retired in good order to seek advice from headquarters.

On the following morning when the farmer arrived to take up his watch, he found that the rail gang had come back in the night, cut both fences and laid track into our property. What's more, they had left the locomotive standing on the intersection. This was just the GTR ploy in reverse, only we made it stick. I suppose the farmer went to a lawyer but I am quite sure that he was fairly treated. I hope so. In any case, he would soon have had his land and his fence returned, as we only wanted the crossing temporarily. We had to get on with our work and let the lawyers settle with the farmer.

I laid out the yard and had a warehouse built with a cubbyhole office and a small stove, and soon materials of all kinds came pouring in, just like up north. To unload and pile all this stuff neatly I was given a foreman and eighty muscular Italians. The foreman was a brawny Irishman called Mike Sullivan who knew his job. He said very little but the navvies delivered ten hours of unstinting labour for him every working day. In the evening they gathered together and sang beautifully, and what they sang was not cheap ragtime but selections from good Italian opera.

I had to keep their time and make up their payroll for the Toronto Construction Company and, when the cheques came in, to deliver them. They were surprised to get their pay in full as they were accustomed to working through a *padronne* who deducted ten per cent for himself.

When it came time for them to move further north, a delegation of three walked down to Bolton and called at my office. One of them made a little speech in broken English and presented me with what looked like a very old and very large gold watch. This was their way of showing appreciation for getting their pay in full. I thanked them but tried to explain that I couldn't accept it for various reasons. I suspected that it was a family heirloom.

During my daily work I had been cultivating my memory training and it came in useful on one occasion.

In railway parlance, any car that does not belong to

127

the road is a "foreign" car. These cars are bound to come in from all over North America loaded with merchandise or produce of some sort, but they are given only a limited time to unload and be returned to their base. Failure to do so is charged to the holding line and a penalty is imposed for every day a car is delayed. This custom is called "demurrage". The system of demurrage goes back to ancient times and applied to ships which had overstayed their docking privileges.

One day we received at the yard a carload of goods in an Illinois Central car, which we unloaded promptly. The eastbound way freight should have picked it up that night.

By chance I happened to be at the Bolton station that evening when an engine and a string of empties pulled in to be coupled on to the train in the siding. I looked over the numbers idly and was surprised that car IC 6071 was not amongst them. The way-freight conductor was a big burly fellow who seemed always to be in a bad humour. Maybe he had dyspepsia, poor fellow. Anyway, I said,

"I see you didn't bring in that IC car."

"It's not there," he growled.

"It's not my concern," I said, "but if you pull into Toronto without that car you are going to hear from the yardmaster."

He turned to the station agent. "Is the car there?"

The agent replied, "If Mac says it's there, it's there."

Going back one mile and switching for that car meant that they would be an hour late getting home, so he was madder than ever, but I was really doing him a favour. He sent a brakeman with the engine running light and I was curious enough to wait for his return. When he did he had the car, so my memory training had served me well.

The winter came but it was very mild and with almost no snow, very different from northern Quebec and northern Ontario with their four or five months of deep snow and spells of below-zero weather.

The whole atmosphere of this little village with its kindly, hospitable inhabitants was what I imagined an English village would be like. The population of Bolton was largely Methodist and they loved to sing, although dancing was forbidden. Nevertheless the girls wanted to dance, so three or four of us undertook to teach them how to do the waltz, the two-step and the polka. The lessons could not be given at home, so we used to walk out to the end of the sidewalk at the Presbyterian Church where there was a wide-open space. Nobody ever came there at night, so under a street lamp, humming or whistling the tunes, they learned the rudiments of dancing.

There were no organized recreational facilities (it was before the days of movies and radio), except in winter when there was a rink made on the frozen Humber River.

I was sweet on a girl at that time but, to my great disappointment, she couldn't skate. I loved to skate and had noticed a girl in a red coat who seemed to float over the ice without any effort, so I took steps to meet her. We hit it off together and I enjoyed many evenings at that rink; I had found myself a lovely girlfriend for the winter, but it never blossomed into a romance.

As in the North, the general contractors at Bolton were Americans (although now they were from Montana), and the bosses were all of English or Scottish ancestry. The latter had formed a new Canadian company called the Toronto Construction Company, which was headed by a man named Dykes.

The general manager was A. B. Cook, former state auditor of Montana and an easy man to get along with. The chief accountant was Harry McLean, a Canadian from Prince Edward Island.

McLean made history a few years later by turning contractor in his own name and building a very difficult line north to Moosonee on James Bay, an arm of Hudson's Bay. In one place he had to divert a river by sending it roaring through a tunnel he had made in a hill of rock.

In time he became very wealthy and retired to a village near Smith's Falls, Ontario. In his retirement years he began giving away his money in cash by the handful. He would proffer bank notes to perfect strangers on the street or throw them out of his hotel window and watch the people scramble for them below. I have no knowledge of his other charities, but no doubt they were generous.

Years later I saw him on Ste. Catherine Street in Montreal. Like so many men of Highland stock he was over six feet in height and broad-shouldered. On this occasion he was wearing a handsome, all-fur coat and a high, round fur cap, so that he looked seven feet tall and resembled one of the old fur barons of Beaver Hall Hill. I had passed him wondering who he was when I remembered an item I had read in the paper about the fabulous Harry McLean, and decided that this must be him. I ran back and touched him on the arm.

"Aren't you Harry McLean?"

"Yes, and aren't you Bert?"

"Yes. I guess we have both changed a bit. I've been through a war since I saw you last, got married and have three children."

He asked after my sister Pearl, whom he remembered from a visit she made to Bolton, and then he suggested that he would give a luncheon at the Mount Stephen Club and get a few friends together, including the author Frank L. Packard, whom Pearl had married. It was arranged for the following day, and Frank and I met some interesting people and heard some fascinating conversation, especially from one American reporter who regaled us with tales of his experiences with Buffalo Bill and Annie Oakley.

When the contractors from Montana moved into our quiet Ontario community, they astonished the natives by hitching six horses to their heavy wagons driven by Westerners in ten-gallon hats.

As soon as grading was finished, we laid track for twenty or thirty miles so that we could use rails for transport instead of unpaved country roads, which were often muddy. In the process the tracklayers stopped at Alliston, a pretty little village at that time.

The tracklayers were living in boarding cars on the siding; they were a pretty rough crowd, although they never made any trouble. The local minister went down to visit them and invited them all to come to church the following Sunday Morning. Privately he wondered if anyone would come, but on Sunday they all turned up, washed and combed and wearing clean shirts and overalls, and occupied the entire gallery. The minister had wisely selected some well-known old hymns and the navvies sang them with a vigour and feeling and evident nostalgia that brought tears to many eyes. Then the minister preached an inspired sermon, and when the plate was passed in the gallery, there were a good many bank notes in it. All of these men were far from home and had not been in a church for years, but I feel sure that the hearts of many were touched that day.

Although we had laid some steel with only a foreman, the job called for a boss tracklayer who would co-ordinate the whole project from trains to labour.

Agate recommended me to Darling for the position although I was only twenty-one, but Darling vetoed the suggestion, saying that I was too young. He may have been right, but I felt that I could do it. Agate's reasoning was that I might be young but that I knew more about it than anyone else he had available. But Darling was adamant. I had been feeling unsettled for some time anyway so, with no other job in sight, and feeling somewhat miffed about not getting a job I knew I could do, I submitted my resignation. I had never liked Darling but that should not have influenced my judgment. His chief did not like him either, so it was only a matter of time before he would go too. As matters turned out he did leave before many months had passed.

I heard long after from an old engineer a strange story about this man. It seems that the CPR was looking for a good division engineer, had heard of a man named Darling, and wrote to him with the result that Darling was engaged. Now it happened that there were two Darling brothers and that one of them was a very competent engineer, but the other was not nearly so capable. The CPR hired the wrong brother.

I decided that I would go into business for myself and wrote to Frank Paget, who replied saying that he was ready to resign and that I should come out west to the Touchwood Hills and confer with him; I had not had a holiday for four years, so I went up to stay with my mother and her sister in Owen Sound and spent two weeks in that pleasant little city with its beautiful surroundings on Georgian Bay.

I may have made a mistake in leaving the company. but I have no regrets. My peregrinating career had led me into several occupations and all parts of Canada except the far North, and I am thankful for the experience.

It was midsummer, 1906.

The world was at peace. The Russo-Japanese War had ended in 1905 in a resounding victory for the Japanese. No wars or rumours of wars troubled the Great Powers. The

132

United States and Canada were growing rapidly in wealth and population. Crops were good and there was a ready market for them. Canada was enjoying a mining boom. It seemed as though peace and prosperity were assured. One could go into business without asking anyone's permission. There were no taxes except land taxes on the property one owned. The income tax had not been invented. There was no sales tax. No one was bothered by having to fill out any government forms. All that was required of anyone was that he paid his debts and that he be honest in his dealings with his customers. It was a good time to go into business. So I went into business.

I have seen Canada grow from a small and weak country of about four and a half million to a prosperous and progressive nation of about twenty-two million, respected by all the nations of the world and having no enemies. She still has internal difficulties to overcome but I feel sure that all true Canadians, English and French and many other races from overseas, who all look on Canada as their home, will strive to understand each other and solve their problems without violence.

And now, near the end of a long life wherein I have been privileged to see much of Canada, I am thankful for my good health and many friends; and I am happy to be living with my wife Marjorie in the beautiful valley and hills of the Gatineau River, very similar to and not far distant from the River Rouge where I worked many years ago.

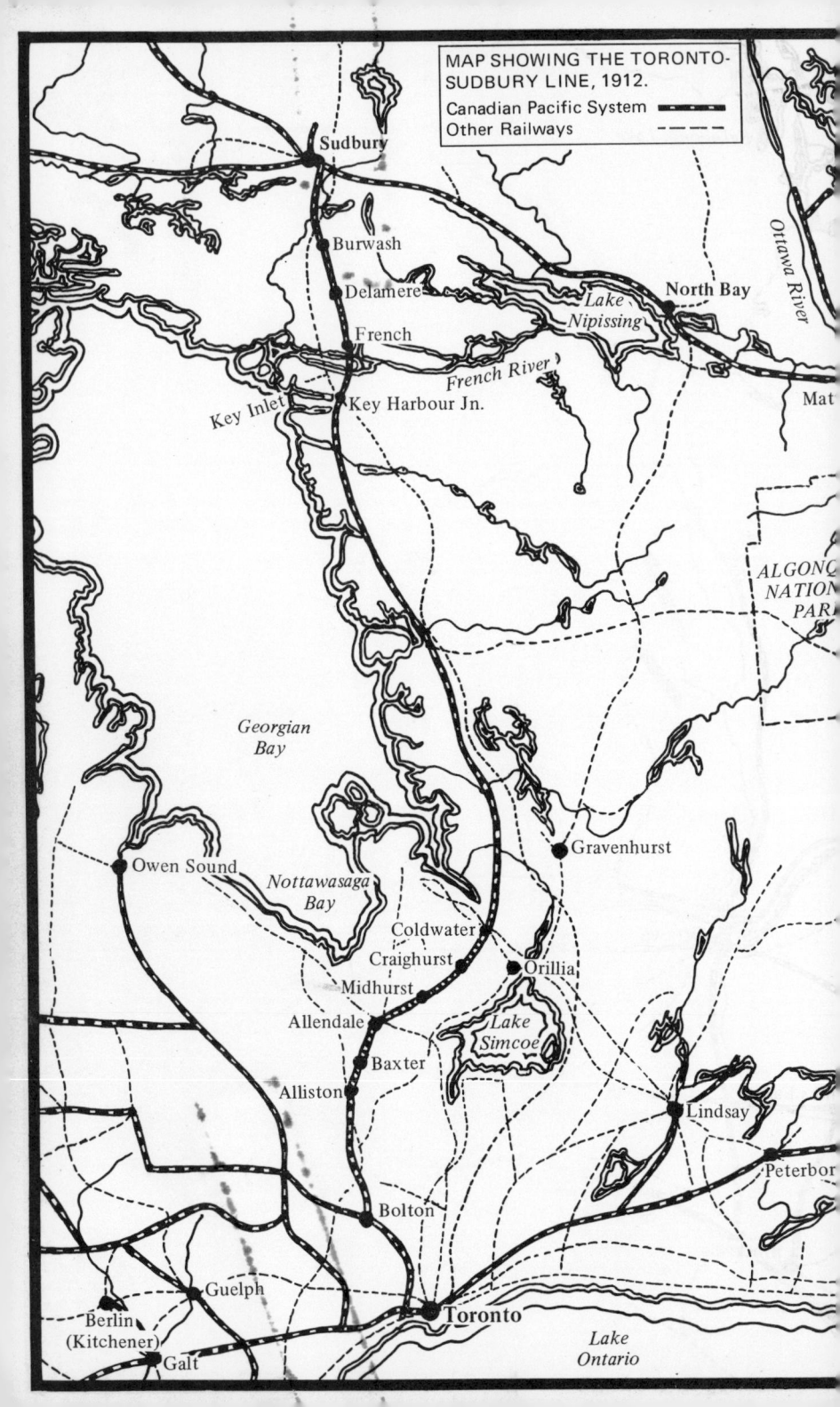

MAP SHOWING THE TORONTO-
SUDBURY LINE, 1912.
Canadian Pacific System ▬▪▬▪▬
Other Railways ▬ ▬ ▬

Sudbury

Burwash

Delamere

French

Key Inlet

Key Harbour Jn.

French River

Lake
Nipissing

North Bay

Ottawa River

Mat

ALGONQ
NATIO
PAR

Georgian
Bay

Owen Sound

Nottawasaga
Bay

Gravenhurst

Coldwater

Craighurst

Midhurst

Allendale

Baxter

Alliston

Orillia

Lake
Simcoe

Lindsay

Peterbor

Bolton

Guelph

Berlin
(Kitchener)

Galt

Toronto

Lake
Ontario